ANXIOUS TO PLEASE

7 REVOLUTIONARY PRACTICES FOR THE CHRONICALLY NICE

JAMES RAPSON & CRAIG ENGLISH

SOURCEBOOKS, INC.®
NAPERVILLE, ILLINOIS

Published by Sourcebooks, Inc.
P.O. Box 4410, Naperville, Illinois 60567-4410
(630) 961-3900
FAX: (630) 961-2168
www.sourcebooks.com

Library of Congress Cataloging-in-Publication Data
English, Craig.
  Anxious to please : 7 revolutionary practices for the chronically nice / Craig English, James Rapson.
     p. cm.
  Includes index.
  ISBN-13: 978-1-4022-0652-8
  ISBN-10: 1-4022-0652-6
  1. Attachment behavior. I. Rapson, James. II. Title.

BF575.A86E54 2006
155.2'32—dc22
                                                        2005033002

Printed and bound in the United States of America.
DR 10 9 8 7 6 5 4 3 2 1

CONTENTS

ACKNOWLEDGMENTS

We are deeply grateful for the impeccable guidance and friendship of our agent, Andrea Hurst, who had the vision and courage to believe in this project and know where it needed to go. Many heartfelt thanks as well for the deft hand and buoyant spirit of our editor, Bethany Brown at Sourcebooks, Inc.

Craig would like to particularly thank Robert and Sema English for a lifetime of love and support, not to mention the writing gene. Muchos gracias to The Commoners writing group (Stephanie Kallos, Ellen Parker, Ron Pellegrino, and Chi Chi Singler) for their honesty, humor, sharp eyes, and tireless work. Lastly, a special thanks to Monica Sweet who not only dreamed the name of this book, but has tested its message day-by-day as a partner, instigator, guinea pig, cheerleader, guru, doctor, deliverer of tea and good cheer, and Transforming Woman.

Many others have contributed to this book and the personal sojourn it represents. We would like to express our appreciation for the support, guidance, and inspiration of the following people:

Shari Barnes, John Bradshaw, Steve Brush, Robert Cumbow, Mary Anne Dorward, Catherine Duke, Dr. Judy Eekhoff, Mike Ferraro and the great folks at Julia's Cafe, Betsy Gilbert, Caryl Greene, Dr. Sarah Groen-Coleyn, Rachel Jay, Stephanie Koontz, Jim Labe and the staff at Teahouse Kuan Yin, Alice Lee, Elizabeth Lyon, Genene Murphy, Janet Page, Shannon Patterson, Denise Silva, Tammy Schlief, Tony Soper, Jim "The Wizard" Strange, Dr. Tim Weber, Bob Weeks, Ted Weinstein, Judith Wills, Dr. David York, Michael J. and Obi-Wan, and Rachel Young.

And a special thank you to all the men and women who so graciously allowed themselves to be interviewed, as well as the many patients and students whose stories have moved and instructed us more than they can know.

Introduction:
An Epidemic of Nice People

The hand moves and the fire's
whirling takes different shapes.
All things change when we do.

—KUKAI

If it were a disease, it would headline newspapers and magazines. There
would be support groups across the country. Telethons would raise money
for research and treatment, an 800-number running at the bottom of the
screen. Public service announcements would detail the list of symptoms so
that people could recognize the condition and seek help as soon as possible:
- Constant anxiety
- Crippled self-esteem
- Depression
- Disruption of family relationships
- Futility in the workplace
- Obsessive thoughts
- Constant need for reassurance
- Undermined romantic intimacy

It is the silent affliction of our day. As many as thirty million people in the U.S. alone suffer from the particular form of anxiety that underlies this condition, even though the condition is both preventable and treatable. It is an epidemic of Nice People.

THE NICE LIST

You may be a Nice Person:

- • If you are always longing for something (or someone).
- • If you feel worried or fretful so often it seems normal.
- • If you often don't know what you want.
- • If you're always thinking about what you wish you had said.
- • If you constantly second-guess yourself.
- • If you apologize frequently, especially for things you are not responsible for.
- • If you take what you're given instead of asking for what you want.
- • If you are often preoccupied with what other people think of you.
- • If you are frequently surprised that other people don't reciprocate your good will.
- • If you do favors for people with the secret hope they will reciprocate.
- • If you are more prone to feel sorry for yourself than to take action and fix a problem.
- • If you tend to give more than you get (you might be resentful about this).
- • If it seems like other people get the attention or the acknowledgment.
- • If it seems like other people get the dates (maybe your friends tell you you're a great catch).
- • If your emotional state mirrors your partner's (if your partner isn't happy, you aren't happy).

THE WAYS AND MEANS OF NICE PEOPLE

Most people are nice, at least part of the time. We live in a world that encourages niceness, even enforces it. A person has to know how to follow the rules, play well with others, and rub folks the right way in order to succeed. It helps if he or she can smile and be gracious under duress.

> At the company picnic, Tom loiters at the edges of a boisterous group, a grin pasted on his face, frequently interjecting an ill-timed quip or a too-long anecdote. Hannah is fussing around the food, making sure there will be enough for everyone and offering help where none is needed. Shelly has been talking for the past hour about Sean, whom she dated a year ago but can't get out of her mind. Roberto has found his familiar place, watching the kids and anxiously monitoring his wife's mood. Dozens more are appeasing, yearning, clinging, and fretting their way through this all-too-typical afternoon.

So what's wrong with being nice? Nothing—in the right context. Being nice makes life more pleasant, and can help things flow more smoothly.

Nice People go further than this. They can't quite help themselves. They *have* to be nice. They are nice whether it's called for or not. They are nice when being ignored or even insulted. They are nice when they want someone (okay, everyone) to like them. They over-function, over-adapt, over-apologize. They navigate their world by accommodating and acquiescing—by trying to please. When things aren't working, they try harder—and most of the time, they're trying harder to be nice.

Nice People are nice whether it's called for or not. They can't help themselves

NICE PEOPLE TRAITS:

- Anxious to please, especially the central people in their life (parent, spouse, girlfriend/boyfriend)
- Show anxiety in relationships by clinging, ingratiating, and over-adapting
- Overly concerned with what others think of them. They are continually surprised when they are rejected
- Don't have good judgment about when to disclose thoughts or emotions, and to whom
- They minimize the faults, flaws, and dangers of people they are attracted to or involved with
- Will often minimize their unhappiness and tell others that they are much happier than they really are
- Are out of touch with the full range of their anger and aggression

THE INNER LIFE OF NICE PEOPLE

While the external appearance of Nice People is characterized by ingratiating compromise, their internal reality is quite different. Nice People suffer from persistent anxiety and fear that often lingers just out of their awareness like the constant backache of the lifelong construction worker. This unsettled emotional baseline is the fount of "nice" behaviors.

EMOTIONAL BASELINE OF NICE PEOPLE:

- Believe that their safety and happiness depend on their ability to please the significant woman or man in their life
- Crave recognition and affirmation of their goodness
- Are often troubled by romantic longings and obsessions
- Use relationships to mask their inability to love themselves
- Idealize others
- Find their own happiness to be elusive and fleeting
- Believe that they will never get what they really want
- Often feel that they have no control over their sexual fulfillment

- Feel contempt for their own Nice Person traits and hate their need for love, affection, reassurance, and sex

> Every morning, Sam goes to get his latte, and Sarah, the barista, always remembers how he likes it. She has a pretty smile and if there aren't too many people around she asks him how things are going. Sam adores Sarah and for the last two years has wanted to ask her out on a date. Some days he imagines the beautiful relationship and rapturous sex that he is sure they would have. Other days he tortures himself with the rejection he anticipates. Some days he skips his latte because he's so angry or disgusted with himself.

THE DAMAGE

We tend to think of a Nice Person as a rather benign character. But the "nice" appearance of Nice People masks the hurt that permeates both their emotional life and their relationships with others. Nice People suffer from frequent anxiety and depression, due in part to the constant neglect of their own needs. Their passive-aggressive behaviors and their difficulty asking for what they want serve to undermine relationships with friends and family members. Not surprisingly, over time these patterns lead to a deadening of intimacy. Nice People are also prone to choosing partners who are not ready for intimacy. Most of the time, these partners are either Nice People themselves, or are on the other end of the scale: demanding, self-involved, manipulative, and domineering.

Sometimes the destruction emanating from the life of the Nice Person can reach severe levels. These outcomes can include eating disorders, substance abuse, self-mutilation, affairs, divorce, and even suicide.

THE HIDDEN EPIDEMIC BEGINS TO APPEAR

A condition this serious should have a dramatic name, a tag that conveys the pervasive loss and heartache that is left in its wake. But the labels we have seem inadequate: Chronically Nice, Anxious to Please, Nice Guy/Nice Girl Syndrome. Even the technical term from the field of psychology is a bit vague: Adult Anxious Attachment. This is an epidemic with an identity problem.

Why has this epidemic gone largely unnoticed? One major reason is that the condition is not usually regarded as a problem. The world is happy to have people who overfunction and doesn't mind that they are motivated by feelings of inadequacy. In fact, many avenues of society rely on the mechanisms of guilt, shame, and fear to manipulate people, and Nice People are the ones most easily manipulated.

The world is happy to have people who overfunction

Nice People themselves are also slow to recognize the damage in their own lives. It would be different if their anxiety appeared one day after a lifetime of confidence and peace. But Nice People have felt this way their entire lives, and most have been denying or dismissing it since they were very young. They often live what Thoreau called "lives of quiet desperation." They are not so severely impaired that they cannot work or marry or function in normal society. They just aren't happy.

Then there are the people who have close relationships with a Nice Person. Spouses, lovers, friends, and siblings are in a complex and typically confusing position. They don't understand why they don't trust someone who is so nice, why they get so mad at someone who is so helpful. The relationship suffers, and they don't really know why.

Despite all of these factors, the epidemic is becoming more and more visible. In recent years there has been a sharp increase in the attention paid to topics like assertiveness training and codependent relationships. Vast numbers of Nice People are now trying empowerment seminars, martial arts instruction, survival skill courses, and inspirational guidance to help them figure out how to overcome the fear that undermines them. Men and women alike are seeking to understand the dynamics that are affecting their relationships and their peace of mind.

THE PATH OF TRANSFORMATION

Nice People yearn intensely for a life that is truly worth living. They ache for an abiding sense of belonging, for an inner peace that can last for longer than a few moments, and for authentic intimacy. They want to find a way to end the cycle of frustration and/or despair. They long to create a rich and satisfying life.

Ultimately, this book is not really about being "nice." It's about hope, healing, and transformation. Throughout this book we use the term Transforming Person to describe a woman or man who is on the path from chronic niceness to a life of strength, kindness, and extraordinary passion.

THE REMARKABLE LIFE OF THE TRANSFORMING PERSON:
- Satisfying relationships with both women and men
- Fulfilling sex
- Solid sense of masculinity and femininity
- Resilient self-esteem
- Happier and calmer emotional life
- Reality-based optimism for the future

To the reader it may seem unfathomable that her or his life can change so dramatically, but rest assured that others have done it, and many more are on the path to transforming their own lives.

The tools for building this new life are the 7 Practices presented in this book. But before employing these practices, we must understand how we became Nice People in the first place.

The Transforming Person is creating a life of strength, kindness, and extraordinary passion

Section One:
Nice People

1

How to Make a Nice Person: The Enduring Effects of Anxious Attachment

Take a puppy away from his mother, place him alone in a wicker pen, and you will witness the universal mammalian reaction to the rupture of an attachment bond—a reflection of the limbic architecture mammals share. Short separations provoke an acute response known as protest, while prolonged separations yield the physiologic state of despair.

—THOMAS LEWIS

...and down they forgot as up they grew.

—E.E. CUMMINGS

IT ALL BEGAN WHEN I WAS A CHILD

The comedian Steven Wright joked that, while he didn't think that being born by C-section had really affected him, "...every time I leave my house I have to go out through the window." Our culture has come to accept the notion that the way we feel and behave is related to the way in which we grew up. It will probably not, then, tie you into knots when we suggest that the psychological roots of the Nice Person originated in his or her childhood.

Nice People come in a wide variety of packages and from quite diverse backgrounds and ethnicities. But they all share a common foundational loss, going back to the earliest days of childhood. From this loss springs the anxiety and fear that drive the Nice Person's behavior.

EMPHASIZING MOTHERS

Recent research shows that fathers are extremely important in raising healthy children. Nevertheless, moms and dads are not simply interchangeable. In this chapter we emphasize the unique role of mothers in establishing the essential, primary bond that supports a baby's development in early childhood.

The loss that we are talking about is the lack of reliable, consistent, and attuned love from the mother (or primary care giver). This loss prevents the formation of *secure attachment*, which is the healthy bond between mother and child.

A LITTLE ABOUT SECURE ATTACHMENT

Like an invisible umbilicus, the bond of secure attachment provides a conduit for the unobstructed flow of emotional nourishment to the child, while similarly allowing for the needs of the child to flow to the mother. When the attachment is secure, the child feels comfortable needing mother and depending on her, and as the baby grows older this comfort can be extended to other caregivers. Eventually, the secure attachment that began with mother will blossom into the self-assuredness that will allow the child to form healthy and openhearted intimate relationships in adulthood.

Secure attachment is the emotional foundation for a calm and confident psyche in the growing child and adult. In order for secure attachment to develop, a baby must believe that his or her mother will:

- Be there when she is wanted or needed
- Be able and willing to provide what the child needs
- Offer love enthusiastically and consistently, without rejection or withdrawal
- Love effectively by staying "in tune" with the child, not being intrusive or demanding

GOOD-ENOUGH MOTHERS

The phrase "good-enough mother" was coined by renowned psychologist and researcher Donald Winnicott to capture the concept that minor failures in parenting, while frustrating for the child, are essential to his development. These small frustrations actually propel him to form an internal representation of his loving mother, which will tide him over during disturbing times. As he grows, this inner resource gets integrated into his personality, making him more resilient and self-reliant.

No mother, of course, can do these things perfectly at all times. Even a woman who is ideally suited for motherhood will have her strengths and weaknesses, as well as her good days and bad days. But research has shown that babies are resilient and will internally compensate for mistakes, lapses, and disappointments.

Even so, the "good-enough mother" has to be reliable enough, responsive enough, attuned enough, and warm enough for the baby to feel securely attached. She must also be able to handle and contain the baby's normal aggression and rejection without withdrawing or retaliating herself. If she cannot reliably do these things, the child becomes anxious and insecure, fearing that this all-important connection with mother is threatened by things

Secure attachment is the emotional foundation for a calm and confident psyche

that are innate in the child: neediness, anger, aggression, and desires to be separate. If things don't improve, this anxiety becomes firmly fixed in the child's body and psyche.

AVOIDANT AND DISORGANIZED ATTACHMENT

At the other end of the spectrum are two attachment styles that represent general failure in the mother-child relationship: *avoidant attachment* and *disorganized attachment*. *Avoidant attachment* is the result of a chronic emotional neglect, and leads a child to routinely reject opportunities for connection and nurture from a parent. Even though these children need reassurance and encouragement, they act as though they don't, and seem unable to be nourished by it even when such comfort is available. As adults they likely will minimize the importance of close relationships.

Disorganized attachment forms when the child is regularly overwhelmed and terrified by the parent. These children face an intense internal paradox: their instinct is to seek soothing from the very parent who is terrifying them. Desperate to maintain a bond with that parent, they fragment internally, repressing their overwhelming rage and fear. When they become adults, these raw emotions will randomly reappear, causing great disruptions in their relationships.

IN BETWEEN WE FIND THE NICE PERSON

In between *secure* and *avoidant/disorganized* attachment is the group of children who get some, but not enough, of what they need from their mother. These children are stuck in a state of perpetual yearning, never getting enough of their parents' nurture to be satisfied. This kind of parent-child bond is known as *anxious attachment*—the one condition that every Nice Person has in common.

There are, of course, many reasons why a mother's care might have been unpredictable. Most of the time, the mother herself received inadequate mothering in her childhood. But even mothers who come from secure attachment can be undermined by a neglectful, abusive, or absent partner.

Research shows that the quality of parenting is also dramatically affected by hardships such as bereavement, illness, and poverty.

Anxiously attached children are unwilling (and unable) to give up their pursuit of the love and connection they so desperately need. Their mothers are typically unpredictable or chaotic, unable to respond with consistent love and attunement. The uneven pattern of care resembles the random feedback pattern of a game of chance, like roulette. This pattern—frustration peppered with random rewards—fosters the sort of compulsion that can be seen in a gambler who will lose large sums of money, but be unable to tear himself away from the casino.

Children raised with this erratic pattern of attunement will often develop compulsive and obsessive tendencies. A child might seem frequently hypersensitive or insecure—unwilling to part with mom, dad, or a beloved object. They may show a surprising devotion to certain minirituals, such as which arm goes in the jacket first, or the exact number of times "I love you" must be said before turning out the light at bedtime. Of course, any child could behave this way from time to time, but what distinguishes anxiously attached children is that they do these things often enough that the behaviors seem to be part of the personality.

It is important to recognize that the adult Nice Person is not an inevitable outcome from these beginnings. A child who experiences anxious attachment early in life may be able to work through and resolve those feelings. A more secure attachment with Mom and Dad can develop if the attention and sensitivity that were missing early on is provided to the child.

Anxious attachment is the condition that all Nice People have in common

Like so many afflictions, anxious attachment is easier to resolve if it's caught early. Unfortunately, the family elements that contribute to problems in early life usually do not change sufficiently as the child grows up. A child who is anxiously attached presents a considerable parenting challenge. Even if the mother has become more stable, the father more available, the family more financially solvent, they are usually not prepared to offer the kind of patient and persistent support that the child now needs in order to restore a secure emotional core.

Regardless of what contributes to the dysfunction of the family, the ultimate effect is that the child does not get the consistent emotional nourishment and containment that is needed. Years later, the child can become an adult whose emotional well-being and resilience have been significantly impaired. The anxious boy or girl becomes a Nice Person.

KINDS OF ATTACHMENT

SECURE ATTACHMENT	ANXIOUS ATTACHMENT	AVOIDANT/ DISORGANIZED ATTACHMENT
Parent is warmly and consistently attuned to baby and contains baby's aggression	Parent not attuned to baby; availability unpredictable or chaotic	Parent is rejecting, emotionally unavailable; or intrusive, terrifying
Child is calm, confident, resilient, and can be soothed when upset	Child is clingy, ingratiating	Child is angry, defiant, withdrawn; or fragmented, overwhelmed
Adult is emotionally well adapted, able to both attach to and separate from others	Adult is anxious, appeasing, overly concerned with what others think, preoccupied with idea of romantic ecstasy	Adult is emotionally shallow, dismissive of connections; or dissociative, frequent intense emotions

NICE PEOPLE ARE ANXIOUS PEOPLE

Nice People may not always look anxious, but they always are. The ability to manage this anxiety varies from one person to the next, and the oscillation of conditions in a person's life will trigger ebbs and flows in anxiety level. Nevertheless, Nice People are anxious people, and whether or not they are conscious of it, this anxiety rules their life.

The Nice Person's relationship with anxiety ranges from a vague uneasiness to a pervasive panic that requires medical attention. Like the desperate, trapped coyote willing to chew off his own leg, the Nice Person will do almost anything to avoid, soften, or extinguish these feelings of anxiety.

What's tricky about the anxiety of Nice People is that it appears to them to be circumstantial. It seems as though there's always something in their life undermining their security, whether it be finances, career, family, dating, school, or whatever trouble *du jour*. Their minds will always be able to point to a few things (or a few dozen things) that are making them fret. But they are unlikely to conclude on their own that they have a chronic condition that prevents them from being able to maintain their calm.

Nice People often attribute their anxiety to a seemingly endless stream of circumstances

It is a disturbing idea that your anxiety might spring constantly, unbidden, from a source within yourself. Nobody wants to believe that there is something wrong *inside* of them. Nice People organize their life around various strategies for relieving their anxiety, hoping to someday get the love that they deeply crave. These strategies are based on the idea that there is something, and especially some*one*, that can give them what they need.

It is, however, a cornerstone of the Nice Person's transformation to begin to recognize that the pain originates from inside, not outside. Transforming People must come to accept that there really is something wrong, something that doesn't work, and something that alienates them from themselves.

To Nice People, this sort of reflection—what some might refer to as a "personal inventory"—may seem impossible. They have spent their lives being preoccupied with what others think and want, and what will make others love them, or at least not reject them. Paradoxically, their preoccupation with others always centers on themselves—worrying about how they are being perceived and feeling guilty about everything.

This kind of thinking is not truly reflective, and so cannot lead to insight and growth. For the Nice Person, the anxious state is overflowing with fretful thoughts that lead them nowhere. For the Nice Person to honestly look behind the curtain of the psyche, she or he will have to develop the capacity to tolerate intense feelings.

FROM GOOD BOYS AND GIRLS TO NICE PEOPLE

The Nice Person concludes early on that love is going to be a difficult prize to capture. Therefore, it becomes imperative to figure out how to be *lovable*.

The anxiously attached child believes that mother's love is a fragile thing that perpetually hangs in the balance

Every young child is interested in learning how to get love, attention, and care. But a securely attached child takes Mommy's love for granted. He will experiment with being coy, demanding, fussy, giggly, and petulant, but does not worry about Mommy's love or responsiveness.

The anxiously attached child, on the other hand, has come to believe that mother's love is a fragile thing that perpetually hangs in the balance. Let's pick up the story of one such child. At the tender age of two, Charlie hopes against hope that he will find a way to secure the love he needs. He urgently wants to find a way to be lovable. As he studies his mother for clues as to what might make him lovable, he learns that she is more relaxed when he is easy (e.g., compliant, quiet, not fussy or demanding), and sometimes this makes her love more available to him. Internally, he resolves to be no trouble and to be a "good boy."

It is at this point that the niceness begins to get entrenched. As "good boy" Charlie grows, he discovers that the world outside works in much the same way. At school and at church, his good behavior is rewarded by smiles, pats, and gold stars, while his bad behavior is frowned upon and punished. The world works this way for all of us, of course, but it has a much greater impact on those who are hypersensitive to rejection and desperate for morsels of kindness. "Good boy" Charlie will devote himself to whatever he considers good deeds, and will encounter little that discourages him from this strategy.

As Charlie grows older, he develops more sophisticated ways to gain favor and avoid rejection. But this is not the only behavior that is defining who he will become. He is also burying his own aggression and neediness, feeding an underground hostility. These are attributes in himself that he comes to detest, as they are (he believes) what prevents him from being loved and cared for. In the years to come, Charlie will feel shame at any hint of their appearance in him—he will insist that he isn't angry, hateful, or needy—and he will hide them from himself as well as the rest of the world. Despite his efforts, these denied emotions will show up in disguised forms in every area of his life.

By his teenage years, Charlie also finds that there is one kind of approval that supersedes the others: the smiling attention of a pretty female. His interest in girls won't make him stand out in a crowd of adolescent boys, but the intensity of his fixation is more enduring, more serious, and more painful than those of his peers. He falls all over himself trying to "nice" his way into the affections of his feminine target. He might even be successful, if only for a limited time. Some girls are quite taken with intensity, and his anxious clinging can be mistaken for passionate fervor. Others may be impressed with his niceness, preferring it to the ill treatment they might receive from the "bad boys." Regardless, the social awkwardness of this

Anxiously attached children are hypersensitive to rejection and are desperate for morsels of kindness

period tends to inflame his overactive sense of shame, and he is prone to problems with depression and low self-esteem.

Eventually, Charlie reaches adulthood and begins to take on the trappings of the adult world. Work replaces school as the organizing activity of his life. He pays taxes, buys a car, votes in an election. He has left (or escaped) home, but his freedom also serves to pique his sense of aloneness in the world. One of his hopeful fantasies is steadily being disproved: getting older is *not* curing him of his anxiety.

The youthful "Nice Guy" Charlie cannot bear the feeling that he is not good enough, yet he also cannot avoid that implication. His anxiety is proving to be intractable, and he finds himself stuck on a treadmill that compels him to keep acting nice, finding only fleeting moments of relief. As a result, his internal alienation and fear continue to pervade his life, often from a place that lies just outside of his conscious awareness. Unconsciously, he plays out his resentment through actions that are passive-aggressive (buying chocolates for his dieting girlfriend) and passive-avoidant (forgetting her birthday altogether).

It is likely that his preoccupation with women, or a particular woman, is growing too. The anxious attachment patterns of his childhood have become fixed in his psyche. The original hope that Charlie could be nice enough to make his mommy love him is seamlessly transformed into the aspiration that he will find his deliverance in the arms of a lover.

ONCE UPON A TIME...

Every Nice Person has a different story, but these stories have similar threads. Consider the implications of the early childhood experience of one girl:

> Little three-year old Tabitha has a mom, Helena, with too much stress in her life. Helena's husband (Tabitha's dad) is traveling on business most of the time, and may be having an affair. The family doesn't make it on his salary, so Helena works part-time to make ends meet. She feels constantly drained by the demands of raising Tabitha and her

five- and eight-year old sisters. She sometimes feels guilty about the relief she experiences when she drops them off at the childcare center. She tries to limit how frequently she leaves the younger kids in the charge of her oldest daughter. Helena's circle of friends has dwindled to almost nothing. She has never been able to rely on her parents, and her mother still spends most of her energy taking care of, and dodging punches from, Helena's alcoholic father.

Most of these details are lost on Tabitha. She knows who daddy is, but doesn't see him enough to understand exactly how he fits into the family. She has ambivalence about her sisters, as their treatment of her varies from warm and loving to harsh and punishing. She loves her mommy more than anything in the world. But sometimes it is really painful to want her so much, and it feels as though the more Tabitha needs her, the more Mommy pushes her away. When Helena is angry, disapproving, rejecting, or distant, Tabitha assumes that she has done something wrong to make Mommy act that way. At three-years old, she is already becoming chronically anxious. To the casual observer, she seems pretty ordinary, even healthy. The supervisor at the childcare center finds her "a bit clingy" and difficult to comfort after her mother drops her off, though that trait hardly stands out in a crowd of toddlers.

Tabitha's mother is not a child abuser or a deadbeat mom. She loves and cares about her kids, but she is overwhelmed most of the time, and is just doing what she can to get through the day.

Tabitha is struggling more than anyone knows. At three-years old she is supposed to be preoccupied with herself and what *she* happens to want in any given moment, but increasingly she is becoming preoccupied with what pleases and displeases her mother. Her stage of emotional development would have her exploring her newly unfolding identity, her sense of separateness from her mother and the rest of the world. This exploration requires that she have an adequate sense of security in her bond with Helena, knowing intuitively that her mommy will continue to love and care for her. But Tabitha does not have that sense of security. The bond with her mother feels shaky, her love uncertain. This insecurity does not bring Tabitha's development to a screeching halt, but it compromises it in ways that can last a lifetime if not resolved.

ANXIOUS ATTACHMENT IN ADULTHOOD

By the time a person reaches adulthood, much of his or her inner world has become solidified. Like a broken bone, the knitting is inevitable, one way or another. For anxiously attached women and men, the internal disturbances that were once fluid and amenable to repair have become set. The way they feel, the way the world seems to work, now falls within the scope of what they would likely call "normal."

Anxiously attached children are often struggling more than anyone realizes

Many adults wrestling with anxious attachment will deny that they are chronically unhappy, and will develop a social persona to support this illusion. The particulars of this persona can be quite complex and varied, from entertaining to helpful to cynical. Frequently, they are coping with a crisis of one sort or another and the emotions of that crisis serve as a cover story for the persistent roiling within. Deep down, they suffer from a secret, unshakable conviction that there is something wrong with them, something shameful. They seek to create a face to present to the world that they imagine will be more acceptable. For many men and women, this becomes the Nice Person persona.

THE INNER LIFE OF THE NICE PERSON

Haunted by feelings of inappropriate guilt and an enduring state of anxious longing, Nice People become preoccupied with the emotional states of those around them, usually without being conscious that they are doing so. This preoccupation can be exhausting. They don't choose to obsess about what others are thinking and feeling; they simply can't shut it off. As with all anxiety conditions, the thoughts, feelings, and fantasies are compulsive, unbidden, and mostly outside of their awareness.

For the Nice Person, relationships become the battleground for warring emotions. This is especially true of romantic relationships, where the levels of emotional intensity and personal meaning are precipitously high, and the resulting floods of emotion tend to overwhelm the capacity for thought and reflection. The Nice Person's anxiety mixes with romance the way alcohol mixes with an argument—amplifying and distorting every emotion and gesture. Love relationships are notorious for dislodging the base of reason in any human being, but normally this condition is short-lived, a harmless flight of fancy, with a more grounded sensibility returning soon enough. For the Nice Person, an entire relationship spanning months or years can be a continuous roller coaster. Usually, this "ride" has destructive consequences for both partners, as well as others (like children) who may be significantly affected by the relationship.

Nice People have learned to survive by "tuning" to the emotional system of the other, and many have remarkable skills in this area. Paradoxically, they accomplish this in part by tuning out themselves.

Anxiety Effects

Guilt: Since anxious attachment begins early in childhood, Nice People have rarely known the experience of feeling relaxed and unworried, and so their emotional baseline is already set to a hyper-aroused state. Often these anxiety symptoms show up as feelings that might not be recognized as anxiety. One example of this is the habit of feeling guilty when guilt is not the appropriate response. Nice People feel guilt

For the Nice Person, relationships become the battleground for warring emotions

about anything that they might feel anxious about: relationships, sex, work, parenting, religion, health, leisure, etc. This ubiquitous guilt can permeate all significant relationships, especially romantic relationships. It manifests in two particular ways:

1. *The apologetic stance:* In this stance, the Nice Person feels and shows apology and shame for almost anything. She or he may, in fact, have the frequent habit of saying "I'm sorry" anytime there is even a whiff of conflict or controversy in the air. Even if nothing is said, body language will likely reveal the trepidation.

2. *The defensive stance:* Here, the Nice Person is reacting to the painful assumption of guilt by being preemptively defensive. He or she has difficulty admitting mistakes and is sensitive to even the hint of criticism. At the same time, the Nice Person is likely to deny that they are angry or even irritated.

Low self-esteem: Nice People are often troubled by feelings of unworthiness and fears of incompetence. They feel they have to demonstrate their value and goodness over and over again, and even though they may be quite competent in social and professional circles they continue to feel shaky about themselves. Their sense of well-being is fleeting; they do not know how to feel at home in the world.

Interestingly enough, the term *self*-esteem is almost a misnomer, because Nice People's insecurity only appears to come from their estimation of themselves. Most likely, they do not know or even care about their own opinion—it's not relevant. What they care about is the way in which others esteem them, a preoccupation that comes from their deepest insecurities. They feel always at risk for rejection and abandonment, and despite all their efforts cannot seem to figure out how to feel secure. Because of this, they do not have a very clear idea of who (or even where) they are; their sense of self is indistinct at best.

At times, a Nice Person will work so hard to suppress their insecurity that it ends up looking like the opposite. It is common for others to perceive the Nice Person as being supremely confident, or arrogant.

Disturbances in Relationships: The anxiety of Nice People is particularly activated by their romantic endeavors. We talk about this in more depth elsewhere (see especially Chapters Three and Nine), but for now we'll simply describe a few of the ways in which Nice People's anxious attachment history plays out in relationships with spouses and lovers.

People need to feel as though they belong, within circles of family, clan, and community. Because Nice People have a very shaky sense of their own belonging, they cannot feel secure in their membership in other circles, even if they know that they are welcome there. To compensate, they tend to over-invest in a romantic relationship and under-invest in other relationships that could be very sustaining for them. In particular, Nice People often neglect their connections to other healthy people of the same gender (see Chapter Seven: Brotherhood and Sisterhood Practice).

> **The more anxious Nice People feel, the less they can see the real man or woman standing in front of them**

Anxiety robs Nice People of their internal resilience—their "emotional immune system"—which would otherwise protect them from the commonplace difficulties of the outside world. Because they have never been able to find a way to feel secure enough, they do not mount a sufficient defense when their well-being is threatened. In their closest relationships, they will accept coldness, abuse, and indifference for a few crumbs of affection. They have great difficulty turning down unreasonable requests and demands, and will choose to do something they will later resent rather than risk conflict. Because of their intolerance of separateness, they will stay too long in relationships that are bad for them. This leads to a myriad of angry and resentful feelings, which are acted out destructively against the self and passive-aggressively toward the partner.

It is important to acknowledge that the life and relationships of Nice People are not always disastrous. Their coping strategies have plenty of merit: they can be patient, gentle, compassionate, and understanding, all traits that tend to nourish closeness. As anxious attachment fades, these same traits will become enormously valuable, combining with independence and strength to make true intimacy possible.

FINDING THE WARRIOR WITHIN

The great football coach Vince Lombardi said that "Fatigue makes cowards of us all." By saying that, he was recognizing the immutable connection between what we feel and what we do. He was describing a circumstance where a person's strength, courage, and perseverance are severely undermined by physical exhaustion.

Similarly, Nice People are constantly being undermined by a debilitating condition, though their affliction is emotional. Despite appearances to the contrary, they are not lacking in strength, courage, or perseverance; these great qualities are getting lost in the quagmire of their anxious hearts.

Anxiety robs Nice People of their "emotional immune system"

Michelangelo once said that David already exists in the unpolished block of marble; the artist's job is to set him free by carving away everything that isn't David. The strong, courageous, and intrepid person lies within, as does the calm, intuitive, and caring person. It may be difficult for Nice People, who have been afraid for their entire lives, to believe that they could one day be relaxed and content, moving powerfully in their career and relationships, and at home in their world. Nevertheless, this kind of transformation is possible.

To begin this transformation, the Nice Person must understand one basic concept: *Recognition of the problem is the indispensable key to unlocking the true character that is trapped within.* This quest is not about changing who you are; rather, it is about finally discovering and unleashing the *real* man or woman that waits within. The following chapters will guide you along the path of awareness and through the challenge of transformation.

2

A Natural History of the Nice Person

No one escapes from their own culture. It's hardwired in us, from birth onward. A consumer society is a consumer society. It may start with washing machines and air-conditioning, but sooner or later we consume each other.

—JOHN BURDETT

We know the driving force behind chronic niceness is anxious attachment. We know that anxious attachment is caused by the disruption of the bond between parents and their children. But why has chronic niceness reached epidemic proportions? There are forces at work in our society that are undermining healthy family structure. Cultural indifference and rapacity, isolation of the family, the speed of change, and environmental stressors, have collided to create an enormous pressure on parents and children, a kind of cultural anvil for hammering the raw materials of an anxiously attached child into an adult Nice Person.

The combination of psychological stress and the dismantling of the extended family safety net have combined to make it difficult for parents to provide sufficient emotional resources for their children. The damaging result: vast numbers of mothers who are undersupported and overworked, and fathers who are physically or emotionally absent—a perfect pot for cooking anxious attachment.

What causes these conditions? If every reader could instantaneously submit an answer to this question, the variety and sheer number of correct answers would be staggering. This chapter will provide an overview of some of the most prevalent social pressures on families. As you read, remember these two touchstones for creating anxious attachment:

1. Mothers who are undersupported
2. Fathers who are absent

OVERVIEW OF SOCIAL PRESSURES

- Losing the Safety Net: Lack of Community, Tribe, and Extended Family
- Dual Careers
- Single-Parent Families
- Working Outside of the Home
- Handing it Down
- Girls
  - Traditional Family Structure
  - Traditional Religions
  - Corporate Structure
  - Harmful and Conflicting Media Messages
  - Commercialization of Girl's and Women's Sexuality
  - Defining Women in Terms of Career and Economic Freedom
  - Superwoman
- Boys
  - Boys Need to Learn Masculinity from Men
  - Feminine Influence in School and Therapy
  - Anger and Distrust toward Men
  - Conflicting Media Messages
  - Validation by Outward Approval
  - Anxiety and Our Environment

LOSING THE SAFETY NET: LACK OF COMMUNITY, TRIBE, AND EXTENDED FAMILY

Most of us no longer live near our families because our society is built to separate us. As young adults, we find that jobs are scarce and the farther we are willing to travel the better our chances become for building a career. And many of us wish to put distance between ourselves and our family. In the past, that was a dangerous and difficult thing to do, so we were more likely to stay home. Today, the Internet allows us to search for jobs and communicate instantaneously with people anywhere in the world. Air travel allows us to reach most destinations on the planet within a day.

For these reasons, it is rare that children grow up with an extended family. At its best, a community of grandparents, siblings, uncles and aunts and cousins provide a cradle of well-being, a support system that can enrich a child's life in a variety of ways. If mother needs to work, there is someone she trusts to watch her baby. If she needs an hour alone to read, to exercise, to nap, for emotional recuperation, she has that option. She has at her disposal the wisdom of other women in her family. If she is single, there are uncles or brothers who will regularly spend time with her children, giving them the male presence that is crucial to their development. Without this diverse support, the "nuclear family" bears the entire responsibility of a child's development and it is a daunting task.

DUAL CAREERS

Economic pressures often require both parents in a family to work outside the home. As a result, it is very common for both parents to be away from their children during a significant portion of the day or night. It is easy to see how this causes erratic decision-making, time pressures, miscommunication, and exhaustion, exacerbating a family's overall level of stress. Here's a sample of the difficulties of dual-career parenting:

- Lack of consistency
- A pervading sense of frantic unease
- Tag-team decision making (no parenting game plan because there is no time to communicate)

- Trading ethics for expediency
- Lack of patience

SINGLE PARENT FAMILIES

The statistics vary—40 percent to 50 percent of marriages taking place right now will end in divorce—but we only need to look at ourselves, our friends, and our families to know that many children are being raised in single-parent families. Single parents tend to be overworked, overstressed, overextended, and overly tired. It is difficult, under these circumstances, to give consistently good parenting. The need for income or companionship often draws the single parent out of the home, making them less available to their children. Conversely, the desire to parent well may keep the single parent at home, leaving them underfunded and constantly worried about money. Without the time for self-care—play, exercise, companionship, or romance—the single parent has no outlet for relieving stress. All of these difficulties translate to anxiety which then seeps into the parent/child relationship.

With the rise of divorce has come an increase in live-in boyfriends and girlfriends, of stepparents, and blended families. While acknowledging that the right stepparent can be a great thing for a child (and may even propel a child toward secure attachment), the inclusion of other adults in the family always requires a period of adjustment. These new situations may disrupt a child's sense of continuity and certainly will cause more anxiety in an already anxious child. A series of new adults in the household will up the anxiety ante correspondingly.

WORKING OUTSIDE OF THE HOME

The onset of the industrial revolution moved the workplace out of the home, taking fathers (and sometimes mothers) out of daily influential lives of their children. With the father no longer at home, the mother once again is alone and often solely responsible for the decisions and responsibilities of day-to-day parenting. A mother's stress level may be increased as she tries (or feels guilty about not trying) to be both a mother and father to her children. Children learn by proximity. Hanging out with mom and dad, even working by their side, was once a wonderful way to learn about becoming an adult.

When a father works elsewhere there can be a sense of psychological distance for both himself and his children. His mind and heart are occupied in a world utterly separate from his household. When he comes home, he is exhausted. Now he walks into a world that has been created and inhabited by his wife and it may seem like a foreign land. The child who spends an entire day in the mother's world and then is confronted by father can experience a similar dissonance, and may take some time to warm up to dad. It takes a very well-balanced man to leave his workplace at the door and merge into the world of his children.

HANDING IT DOWN

Before we talk about the pressures that kids face, it is important to remember that anxiety, like any other family trait, can be handed down from generation to generation. Take, for example, the son of a war-scarred and emotionally absent father who becomes a Nice Guy (in part) because he so desperately wishes for his father's love. This Nice Guy, in turn, gets married. He is obsequious with his wife, always trying to please, and never taking a stand. This is the style of marriage that he models for his son. When the son gets married, there's a good possibility that he will build the same Nice Guy model.

You can substitute a mother and daughter in this story. You can make the story about poverty, alcoholism, deadbeat dads, or sickness. In fact, you can make this story about health, courage, emotional openness, love of the clarinet, and playing catch at the park. The point is, the quality of our lives and parenting (including anxiety) is handed down to our children who hand it down to their children.

CULTURAL INFLUENCES ON BOYS AND GIRLS

While the stresses of modern life are visited upon both girls and boys, our society is curiously gender-specific when it comes to some of the particular effects of anxiety. The following paragraphs discuss some of these differences.

Cultural Influences on Girls

The pressure our society puts on Nice Girls can be oppressive. Traditional influences urge unhealthy self-sacrifice and chronic niceness as a pathway to femininity. Girls who attempt to break the bonds of niceness are often punished. Simultaneously, the culture often demands that women achieve self-realization exclusively through career and economic freedom. For the Nice Girl, who has a desperate sense of longing for relationship, this kind of hyper-independence creates a deep conflict.

TRADITIONAL FAMILY STRUCTURE

There is a traditional family structure in many parts of our culture in which girls are expected to support boys, and women are expected to provide the underpinnings that hold all the family together. In many families it's okay for boys to leave their socks everywhere, but not for girls to do the same. Teenage boys may be expected to occasionally break windows, break wind, drive too fast, drink too much, and have sex, but this kind of behavior is unacceptable for girls because it is unseemly, unfeminine, and not nice. The limelight also belongs to boys, giving the family a sort of football game structure in which the girls are expected to cheer their brothers, fathers, and uncles from the sidelines, smile prettily, and otherwise remain quiet. The message is clear: being nice is feminine and it wins approval for the girl. For the anxiously attached girl, this is a powerful incentive. While the inequities of this family model have been addressed extensively by feminist (and later on by mainstream) writers, it remains firmly in place.

TRADITIONAL RELIGIONS

The traditional family model above is often inextricably linked to traditional religion. Many traditional religions teach girls that it is their duty to submit and support, while also stifling their own desires and ambitions. As these girls become wives and parents, this behavior becomes a kind of maternal martyrdom in which a woman sacrifices her sense of self for her family and friends. These Nice Girl teachings are hard to detect because they are blended with healthy spiritual practices such as service and humility. It is particularly hard for the girl who is anxiously attached to separate which messages are healthy and which are not.

CORPORATE STRUCTURE

Our society's male-dominated corporate structure presents women in the workplace with some very difficult decisions. While progress has been made, there is still a great deal of pressure for women to choose "feminine" professions—jobs that are indoors, relatively safe, and require a giving and supporting nature. These professions might be ideal for the women who are drawn to them *if* they didn't offer less money, benefits, and status: secretaries, teachers, and nurses versus engineers, administrators, and doctors. Of course, there are more and more women engineers, doctors, and principals, but they can expect to be greeted with a variety of obstacles along their career path—derision, skepticism, harassment, pressure to emulate a masculine style. Society sends a clear message to women in the workplace: Be a Nice Girl and we will approve of you (though we will not pay you well); try to be anything else and we will make it tough on you.

HARMFUL AND CONFLICTING MEDIA MESSAGES

Our consumer culture has a bottomless appetite and a protean ability to shift shapes. It can take in any ideal, fad, theory, or fact and turn it into a money-maker. The messages are relentless as jackhammers, but utterly without substance or direction. They are also wildly contradictory. A girl or woman is told that she must:

- Make her own living *and* rely on a man
- Be in charge of her own sexuality *and* subjugate herself to a man's pleasure

- Be aggressively successful *and* be pleasingly submissive
- Command attention *and* defer the limelight
- Run a business *and* run a household
- And above all, she must look good while she's doing all these things.

In other words, a girl must purchase her validation to gain the outward approval of men, of other women, and of the culture. These conflicting messages are poisonous enough for any girl or woman trying to find her own truth, but for a Nice Girl, whose prime motivation is the anxiety to please, they can be lethal.

COMMERCIALIZATION OF SEXUALITY

The commercialization of women's sexuality has a particularly strong influence on Nice Girls. Nice Girls have a bone-deep need to make people like them. They also have a propensity to make unconscious deals with their romantic partners: "I'll flatter you if you'll love me," "I'll worship you if you'll treat me well," "I'll please you if you don't leave me." (See Chapter Three: Pedestals, Altars, and Gilded Cages.) These same girls and women are being bombarded by constant images of sexuality and body image for sale: commercials (buy this lipstick and men will adore you); magazines (42 ½ Secrets for Keeping Your Man); celebrities with smaller hips, bigger lips, smaller noses, bigger breasts; and everywhere signs that say "Slim Down" or "Buff Up." These messages ratchet up the already tightly wound anxious state of the Nice Girl by hitting her where she lives ("Do people like me?" or "What are they thinking of me?" or "When will my prince come?"). She may choose a message (for instance, "Men like girls who appear sweet but are nasty in bed") and pursue that course as a means of getting love, regardless of her own preferences and needs. Or she may become so overwhelmed by the plethora of products and trends that she gives up the possibility of a relationship because "it's all too difficult." In either case, she is ignoring her true self, while her propensity for giving up her body and her integrity in exchange for approval is deeply reinforced.

DEFINING WOMEN IN TERMS OF CAREER AND ECONOMIC FREEDOM

The women's movement sometimes defined women in terms of career and economic freedom *from men*, a concept which moved into the culture at large and was embraced by many women. While this kind of identification is quite a useful tool for combating the gender limitations of society, it is a hopelessly narrow way to define a woman's life and being. Humans need relationships. Many women have a strong desire to be mothers and mates. Nice Girls who have adopted this economic definition of self-worth find that their own personal longing contradicts the values they are trying to assume. As a result, they feel ashamed of themselves. Until a Nice Girl is well on her way to transformation and has learned which part of her need for relationship is healthy and which part is unhealthy, it will be very difficult for her to weigh the relative importance of avocation, family, romance, and career.

SUPERWOMAN

Just as the women's movement began to define a new kind of strong woman who is independent from a man, the culture devoured her and spit out the icon of the Superwoman. This new feminine ideal is no more realistically attainable than a comic book hero, but she is a perfect vehicle for selling products. The Nice Girl aspiring to be Superwoman must be a gifted mom, a corporate dynamo, a sexual tigress, and a supporting wife. Superwoman operates like a paper doll: you have to buy all of the outfits to dress her up, and if you're missing one of the outfits you're going to be the laughingstock of the neighborhood. In the 1970s, Enjoli perfume gave the public the image of three women, one in a smart dress with a shopping bag, one in a bathrobe with a frying pan, and one in a slinky evening dress, all armed with microphones and singing the following lyrics.

I can bring home the bacon...
Fry it up in a pan...
And never ever let you forget you're a man,
'Cause I'm a WOMAN...with Enjoli

Superwoman is designed to induce an anxiety in women that impels them to buy things. The marketing strategy has worked alarmingly well and Nice Girls are particularly vulnerable to Superwoman's powers.

Cultural Influences on Boys

One of the most damaging influences on boys is the absence of personal contact and influence with fathers and other men. When combined with the highly conflicting models for masculinity that our culture serves up, boys find themselves pressured, uncertain, confused, and anxious.

BOYS NEED TO LEARN MASCULINITY FROM MEN

As we have seen, men are often emotionally or physically absent from the home, and this means that boys are learning about masculinity from their mothers. A mother's influence is obviously crucial to a boy's development. However, masculinity is a way of being in the world that is passed along from men to boys.

Not a single one of us [referring to a group of men] felt that our manhood had come from our mothers. They nurtured, comforted, educated, and sang to us; they nursed us when we were sick, taught us manners, and protected us from various things, including the abuses of our fathers. But they couldn't teach us how to become men.

—AARON R. KIPNIS, PHD,
KNIGHTS WITHOUT ARMOR

Boys who learn about masculinity primarily from a woman, even if she is a wonderful and well-intentioned mom, receive a feminine perspective of what a man should be, or just as often, what a man should not be. If the woman has had too many negative experiences with men, her fear or anger will be communicated in a thousand little ways. Without the grounding presence of a healthy man to mitigate these messages, there is a cumulative negative effect. It may not be until adulthood that a man notices that he is ashamed to have a man's feelings and a man's body—that he feels guilty being a man.

A boy is full of flights of fancy, rambunctiousness, rude humor, sweetness, violence, outrageousness, and contemplativeness. Later on, nature will dramatically increase the dosage of testosterone to this mixture. It is only by spending time with a father or another good man that a boy learns to appreciate his innate maleness. From a good father he learns to harness his maleness with restraint, patience, resolve, and integrity.

A boy cannot learn masculinity from his mother

FEMININE INFLUENCE IN SCHOOL AND THERAPY

The lack of masculine input is reflected in schools where the majority of early education teachers are women. Furthermore, the teaching methods of our public schools are ill-suited to the way many boys learn. Recent research has shown that girls' and boys' brains develop and function very differently, resulting in boy-behaviors that are considered inappropriate and even offensive in the modern classroom. Once again a boy is subliminally being told that his gender is shameful.

Similarly, men may have difficulty finding therapies which are particularly suited to the way they process. When a man walks into a therapist's office, he finds the same "verbal-emotive" model that turned him off in school. In other words, he will be sitting and talking. Furthermore, men have been taught that it is not manly to be introspective or to seek any kind of help at all. Nice Guys, as much as any, have bought into this way of thinking.

ANGER AND DISTRUST TOWARD MEN

There is a general cultural climate of anger and distrust toward men. Television often portrays men as either inept buffoons or murderous machines. It has been suggested and defended in our culture that war, rape, and dominance are part of the essential male makeup. But it isn't difficult to look at the men around us—our brothers, friends, uncles, fathers, and sons, and indeed the vast majority of men—to know that this is not the case. The demonizing of the male is a particularly harmful stereotype perpetuated by our culture.

For boys who are anxiously attached, these negative reflections send a powerful message: "There's something wrong with me for being a boy. I'll try to make up for it by being as nice as I possibly can." In fact, many Nice Guys try to make up for it by hiding their maleness. The contemporary woman's ubiquitous cry of "Where are all the real men?" is in part a product of Nice Guys hiding their strength, their libido, and their sense of belonging to and in the world.

CONFLICTING MEDIA MESSAGES

And all the while the culture is sending utterly conflicting messages. Tough guys, solitary guys, emotionless guys—media characters like the Marlboro Man and James Bond; the personas of actors like Clint Eastwood, Arnold Schwarzenegger, and Vin Diesel; rappers like Eminem and 50 Cent; and too many rock stars to name—these are heroes that school boys emulate. After all, on the screen they get the girls, don't they? What is devastating to the Nice Guy about these mythic heroes is that they *don't care* whether they get the girl. In fact, it is quite clear that caring is a sign of weakness and to be despised. Nice Guys find their own need emasculating, and they hate themselves for it.

VALIDATION BY OUTWARD APPROVAL

But some of the men fathomed that there was yet one more level within, a betrayal deeper than that of personal or public male elders...Its tsunami force...had washed all the men of the American Century into a swirling ocean of larger-than-life, ever-transmitting images in which usefulness to society meant less and less and celebrityhood ever more...even the most traditional of craftsmen and community builders lived in a world where personal worth was judged in ornamental terms: Were they "sexy"? Were they "known"? Had they "won"?

—SUSAN FALUDI, *STIFFED*

One of the most enduring qualities of masculinity is the need to have meaningful work. Work, as much as family, anchors and validates a man. But our culture has created an environment in which boys and men are no longer validated for doing good work—work that benefits family and community.

This environment can leave the Nice Guy, who is already questioning his masculinity, feeling utterly lost. In response, some Nice Guys put on a hard-hearted bastard "disguise," and start reaching for the accepted social values (the car,

Men need meaningful work

the clothes, the ladder-rung job, the fifteen minutes of fame). But more often, they just try harder and harder to be a team player on a team that will abandon them at the slightest economic impulse.

Between the lack of male influence and the conflicting messages of the culture, Nice Guys find themselves floundering. Without solid models for masculinity, they try to cope by asserting their childhood model for survival—being nice. The results are painful, numbing, and emasculating.

ANXIETY AND OUR ENVIRONMENT

Our environment has changed radically and we are exposed to a myriad of anxiety-producing stresses that were less prevalent or nonexistent in the past. Environmental stress affects people differently, partly because each person's environment is different and partly because each person's sensitivity is different. Take a look at the following lists of recently minted anxiety producers to find out how greatly you might be affected.

See the questionnaire on the next pages:

LOW STRESS				HIGH STRESS	CITIES
1	2	3	4	5	Noise pollution (traffic, construction, aircraft, yelling, amplified music, etc.)
1	2	3	4	5	Light pollution (too much light during sleeping hours)
1	2	3	4	5	Crime
1	2	3	4	5	High-speed travel (highway driving, airplanes)
					CHANGE
1	2	3	4	5	The pace of change (future shock or the inability to cope with the pace of change)
					TECHNOLOGY
1	2	3	4	5	Consumer assault (unrelenting advertising)
1	2	3	4	5	Television and computer viewing (eye strain, headaches, etc.)
					WORK
1	2	3	4	5	Work environment (increased hours, repetitive stress, deadlines, criticism)
					FOOD
1	2	3	4	5	Sugar

1	2	3	4	5	Caffeine
1	2	3	4	5	Processed foods (artificial sweeteners, dyes, preservatives, enriched products, added chemicals, chemically deconstructed and reconstructed, does not provide nutrients or fiber)
1	2	3	4	5	Tobacco (preservatives and pesticides)
					PHARMACEUTICALS
1	2	3	4	5	Prescription drugs
					PHYSICAL CONDITION
1	2	3	4	5	Lack of sleep
1	2	3	4	5	Weight issues
1	2	3	4	5	Chronic pain
1	2	3	4	5	Chronic medical condition

If you answered each question above, your cumulative total score will fall between 17 and 85. Any single item scoring 3 or higher is really worth looking at with an eye toward making whatever change might be possible. A cumulative total greater than 35 suggests that your environment is driving up your overall stress level; a total greater than 50 means that these stressors may be taking a serious toll on your health.

WHEN CULTURE IS JUST THE THING THAT GROWS ON THE YOGURT AT THE BACK OF THE FRIDGE

This chapter was an overview of some of the pressures in our society that shape Nice People. While it may feel overwhelming to be reminded of the daily anxiety we face, it is also part of the road to strength, joy, and contentment. If we are unaware of how society is affecting us, we can do nothing about it. The very act of recognizing our difficult childhood and daily anxieties—that "aha" moment when we think, "Yes, that's me, that's how it is!"—is the beginning of transformation.

There is one more stop along the way before we get to the 7 Practices. We need to examine the hidden thought processes and feelings of Nice People in romantic relationships.

3

Pedestals, Altars, and Gilded Cages

Pedestal: A platform for an object of worship

Altar: A place of sacrifice

Gilded Cage: A prison designed to keep its prize confined through the use of seduction and emotional entrapment

I don't have relationships; I take hostages.

—FAMILIAR SAYING IN TWELVE-STEP GROUPS

I don't know why things didn't work out—we had so much in common. We both loved him and hated me.

—UNKNOWN

While anxious attachment affects virtually every part of the adult Nice Person's life, its effects are most pronounced in one area: romance.

A romantic relationship can represent the polarities of heaven and hell for anyone. There is nothing quite like the bliss of feeling loved and wanted, nor the excruciating pain of being rejected by one's lover. These intertwining themes of romance—magical redemption and tragic loss—have been ubiquitous storylines since Adam and Eve.

For Nice People, these dramatic extremes can be a regular, even daily, occurrence. The dynamic of "he loves me, he loves me not" is part of an internal roller coaster that leads to Nice behaviors such as apologizing and acquiescing.

THE PEDESTAL—IDEALIZING THE LOVER

We all wish for perfection, wholeness, and ecstasy. From time to time we will project those wishes by idealizing someone, whether that person is a lover, a teacher, a parent, or someone we know only from a distance. Usually these idealizing fantasies pass away quickly enough as we encounter the realities of the other person's limits and foibles.

Idealization is typical of new romances. Lovers look at each other with the rosiest of lenses, hearts soaring with improbably high hopes. They feel as though they have discovered the grandest love of all time, and they may be stricken with a profound sense of destiny in having finally found their true soul mate.

For most couples, this romantic conflagration begins to calm after a short period of time, the idealized projections having been supplanted by real experience with the other mortal in the partnership. Sometimes the fire simply burns itself out, and the relationship either ends or continues indefinitely in a bland and autonomic fashion. In the best of relationships, the couple learns to tend and care for the fire, using it skillfully for warmth and sustenance; for them, the fire of romance becomes something that serves, rather than defines, their union (see Section Three).

Nice People tend to cling stubbornly to their idealizations, particularly when it comes to the realm of romance. They feel that they "must have" a lover who can be truly adored, whose exalted status makes their love for the Nice Person a magical experience. They feel as though an ordinary partner, an ordinary relationship, won't be enough to satisfy them.

This idealization is, of course, unfair to the human being who is being deified. This man or woman cannot live up to such a high billing, and eventually begins to cringe under the weight of inflated expectations.

Unfortunately, Nice People have great difficulty tolerating the disillusion-ment of their myth (see Chapter Nine, Disillusionment Practice), and will often go to great lengths to perpetuate it. They will persistently cling to the idealized view of their lover, and will react with denial and even rage when confronted with the other's imperfections and differences.

It is important to understand that Nice People generally don't know when they are idealizing, are thoroughly resistant to knowing that they are idealiz-ing, and will often be quite defensive if confronted about it. The reason is at once simple, confusing, and devastating: Nice People can't bear the pain and fear that is evoked by being intimate with a *real* person, and so they idealize them. Real people can be selfish, aloof, insensitive, and boorish. Real people can leave.

Nice People are desperate for the kind of unshakeable security that they needed and didn't get in childhood. Since adult romance doesn't offer that kind of security, Nice People develop fantasies about their lovers and potential lovers. They unconsciously idealize, crafting a pedestal designed to keep the frightening reality at bay. Over time, the pedestal creates distance and artifi-ciality in the relationship, undermining the very security that is longed for.

Peter and Shannon were both in their mid-twenties when they met as members of the same wedding party. By chance (he would say "fate") they were paired to walk the aisle together during the processional, and he wished the rehearsal could have gone on all night. At the rehearsal dinner, they discovered that they shared an interest in water skiing and Eastern philosophy. He thought she was the most beautiful woman he'd ever seen, and couldn't help imagining her walking down that same aisle, wearing the white dress this time, to promise her eter-nal love for him. The wedding event had an enchanting effect on Shannon, too. She was attracted to Peter's boyish grin and gentle demeanor; so she was more than pleased when he called a few days later to ask her out.

It is now six years later. Peter and Shannon have dated, gotten engaged, broken up, gotten back together, and have managed to get married amid much turmoil and conflict. Shannon, unsure of what she wants to do with her life, has recently begun to research graduate schools.

Today, Peter has surprised her by announcing that he has given notice at the Parks Department and has accepted a position with an investment firm. He explains that, although it means giving up a job that he loves, it is worth it because now he can afford to support her while she goes back to school. Shannon feels uncomfortable with Peter's grand gesture, but isn't quite sure why. She thinks she should feel grateful, fortunate to have a husband who is so generous. Instead, she feels a vague sense of guilt and obligation. She also feels numb to his apparent affections and, oddly enough, feels a little contemptuous of him. Peter, who had secretly hoped for a bigger response from her, covers his disappointment with a smile and asks if she wants some tea.

At first, Shannon felt as though she was getting the kind of admiration and focus that she really needed and desired—it can be quite nice to be the recipient of such high esteem. She basked in the glow of Peter's enthusiastic attentiveness.

Compliments from a Nice Person can feel like applause from a drunken audience

Now, however, being the object of Peter's adoration can make her feel like, well, an object. Peter is adoring the Goddess that he projects onto Shannon and often doesn't see her as she really is. It feels hollow to Shannon, and she doesn't quite understand why.

Peter's unconscious idealizations (called "projections" in the parlance of psychoanalysis) operate like a cheap air freshener, aiming to neutralize and obscure anything that *might* be malodorous. Peter wouldn't say that Shannon is perfect, but he would frequently credit her with having pure thoughts and noble intentions when the truth is something less than that. If she fails to keep an agreement, treats him poorly, or speaks contemptuously to him, he is likely to tell himself that he must have had it coming, or that he misunderstood her meaning.

SPOTTING THE PEDESTAL

You may be putting your partner or prospective partner
on a pedestal...

- if it seems like life without them would be dull and meaningless
- if you place a supreme value on their positive traits
- if you tend to excuse or rationalize their bad behavior
- if people you trust don't hold a similar high opinion of them
- if you sometimes get intensely angry when their behavior doesn't fit your view of them
- if you frequently wonder what they see in you

Nice People specialize in romantic projections, whether the person is a long-term partner or someone they just met. A husband's lack of social skill is covered up by "still waters run deep." A girlfriend's habit of intrusion is edited down to "she just cares a lot." Good traits are exaggerated with "she is the most..." and "he is the best..." Significant others aren't thought of as being flawless, but they are seen through rose-colored glasses.

THE ALTAR—SACRIFICING TO PLEASE

When Peter decides to give up a job that he loves, he is making a sacrifice that he justifies in the name of love. After all, Shannon is his beloved, and of course love requires sacrifice, doesn't it?

Peter doesn't just believe in the motto "Love hurts"—he champions it. He fully expects that his relationship will require him to give up things that are important to him, and sometimes he is almost eager to go through pain and loss in order to demonstrate his true devotion to Shannon.

Peter believes his "eagerness to give" is a sign of his ardent love for Shannon. In truth, it is a sign of his intense need to feel secure. His subterranean hope is that his grand sacrifice will make Shannon feel further indebted to him, thus providing more insurance against her leaving him. Shannon is the Goddess, and his conviction is that she should provide him with the security he wasn't able to get from his mother and father; he believes that is what relationships are supposed to be all about.

Peter turns to the tool that he knows: Niceness. If he is insecure or in pain, needs comfort or reassurance, he will be nice, hoping that his niceness will buy him some love. If that doesn't work, he will try harder to be nice. He becomes super-nice, mega-nice, turbo-nice.

But this niceness isn't designed to make Shannon feel good; it's designed to make her feel indebted. For this reason, Peter's gratuitous niceness eventually takes on the form of sacrifice. As it has been since childhood, he is quite willing to suffer indignity and self-neglect in service to the greater need for security. It's an implicit trade agreement, but the terms of the agreement are never expressed, and Shannon isn't given much of a choice. Peter is desperate to control Shannon's affections and repeatedly attempts to entrap her with obligation.

THE SACRIFICE FACTOR

In their book, *All the President's Men*, authors Bob Woodward and Carl Bernstein relate an anecdote about G. Gordon Liddy. Liddy was at a party and at one point demonstrated his toughness by holding his hand over a candle flame until his flesh was burning. Someone asked him, "What's the trick?" Liddy responded, "The trick is not minding."

As chilling as that may sound, it is very much the dynamic involved when Nice People make sacrifices. They can have a callous neglect for their own emotional well-being, "not minding" that they may be enduring unnecessary pain and damage in the hope of garnering the affection or approval of another. The primary difference with Liddy is that he was completely conscious and intentional about his indifference to the damage being done to his hand; Nice People are rarely aware of the ways in which they leave themselves vulnerable to harm.

Nice People have a diminished capacity to treat themselves as worthy of being cherished

Nice People have a diminished capacity to treat themselves as worthy of being cherished. In Peter's case, a powerful protest should have arisen within him that said, "Wait a second, this is a great job that I should hang on to. This is not a strong enough reason to quit. I can't do that to myself!" But that feeling, if it comes at all, appears only as a weak protest, easily overpowered by Peter's need for Shannon's affections. He cannot bear the fear that he will lose her love.

THE GILDED CAGE—LOVER AS CAPTIVE

Peter, Peter, pumpkin-eater
Had a wife and couldn't keep her
Put her in a pumpkin shell
And there he kept her very well.
—MOTHER GOOSE

When Nice People find a love relationship that they want to keep, excitement is usually accompanied by a growing unrest, a deep fear of losing the loved one. This fear stays largely hidden, and it falls to the unconscious mind to try to ensure that the lover won't leave. Without being aware of what they are doing, the Nice People begin to assemble a Gilded Cage for their mate.

> Third grader Sasha wants Madaleine to be her friend. At lunch, she offers Madaleine her cupcake, and when the "gift" is accepted, Sasha announces, "Okay, now we're best friends."

Sasha has made an awkward attempt at creating a Gilded Cage. From the perspective of eight-year-old Madaleine, it may feel like she has suddenly found herself in a committed relationship from which there is no escape.

The Gilded Cage dynamic is basically the same for Peter and Shannon as it is for Sasha and Madaleine, even though the elements of the adult pairing are much more complex. The relationship between Peter and Shannon features genuine love and caring, but it also features a Gilded Cage that has been under slow and steady construction for several years now. The golden bars in this cage include:

- **Dependence:** Shannon is financially dependent on Peter, more so if she goes back to school or has a child.
- **Isolation:** Shannon's time has progressively become monopolized by the relationship, diminishing her connections to friends and family.
- **Indebtedness/Obligation:** Peter's "generous" and continual sacrifices leave Shannon feeling indebted to him, and their unwritten contract is that she owes him her devotion in return.
- **Guilt/Shame:** Peter's defensiveness and chronic niceness enforce the stance that he is never to be blamed for anything; Shannon feels guilty if she gets mad at him, and feels like a complete bitch if she secretly imagines leaving the marriage.
- **Pity:** Peter has made sure that Shannon knows how completely crushed he would be if he thought that she might not want to be with him.

These "golden bars" are essentially contracts between partners, with both people playing a role in the creation of the Gilded Cage. Though the contracts are unspoken and unconscious, they may feel more binding than the official wedding vows. Each person has an expectation for what they will give and what they are entitled to get in return. Nice People tend to have the same basic expectations in their relationships: "I will overfunction, make sacrifices, and be scrupulously correct. You will never blame, reject, or abandon me." The partner may or may not share this expectation, but they will feel the pressure to abide by it.

It is worth noting the near-invisibility of the Gilded Cage. The dynamics in Shannon and Peter's relationship (dependence, isolation, indebtedness/ obligation, guilt/shame, and pity) have occurred without either of them noticing. The contracts have formed without any discussions or conscious consent.

THE PROMISE OF UNCONDITIONAL LOVE—THE STRONGEST BAR IN THE GILDED CAGE

> Oh, love's best habit is in seeming trust...
> **—WILLIAM SHAKESPEARE, "SONNET 138"**

When people imagine the highest form of love, they frequently use the term "unconditional love." We say that God loves us unconditionally, and that a mother and father should love their child regardless of any conditions that can be imagined.

Often a couple will say that they, too, will love one another unconditionally. There are strong hints of this in the familiar marriage vows: "…in sickness and in health, for richer and poorer, 'til death do us part." Particularly for Nice People, this can mean that the partners will love each other forever, no matter what happens, and no matter what the other person does.

This promise should give us considerable pause. We cannot truly afford to say that it doesn't matter what happens or what the other person does. We can all think of extremes of violence and betrayal that should lead to the end of a relationship, even if it is difficult to determine precisely where that line is. But regardless of where the limits are, our commitment is not truly unconditional. So why would we say that it is?

For Nice People, this vow of unconditionality is an attempt to erase the fears from anxious attachment, to manufacture the secure bond that was missed in childhood. The promise of unconditional love, then, can become the strongest bar in the Gilded Cage. It is nearly irresistible, like the promise of a lifesaving treatment to a dying man. It can be as insidious as a Trojan horse, welcomed without resistance into the emotional depths of one's heart.

> On the other hand...
>
> There are many good reasons for making a marriage (or other long-term) commitment. The conventional vows that were cited earlier can be said with a healthy intent, as a way of expressing a couple's shared vision for a relationship that is being designed to withstand the challenges and insults that life invariably presents.

A HEART DIVIDED—THE GODDESS/PRINCE CONSTRUCT

As we described in Chapter One, anxious attachment occurs because a person has had contradictory kinds of early childhood attachment experiences: i.e., sometimes the needed love and attunement was available, sometimes it came at a cost, and sometimes it wasn't anywhere to be found. She or he couldn't forget the joy and relief of getting the right kind of love, but also couldn't forget the terrible pain of not getting it. The child wasn't able to reconcile these two experiences and so became "split" internally. The anxious child grew up and became a Nice Person, with the internal split buried deep inside.

This internal split involves holding on to both sides of a contradiction without letting go of either side. The Nice Person simultaneously believes:

1. "A great love will cure my anxiety and make life worth living;" and
2. "Sooner or later I will be mistreated, rejected, and abandoned."

Nice People don't know how to reconcile these two beliefs, and yet they find it impossible to expunge either of them. If they lean into the dream of a magical romance, they are quickly pierced by the conviction that their dream guy or girl will eventually be dismissive and punishing. If they try to force themselves to simply accept that they're doomed to an endless trail of disappointments and hurts, the irrepressible hope for an idyllic relationship will dangle temptingly once again.

> When Peter and Shannon had been dating for about six months, they took a vacation together at a nearby beach resort. One morning Shannon told Peter that she was going to take a hike up the coast. Peter asked if she wanted his company, and was crestfallen when she said that she just felt like going by herself. He managed a weak smile and said that he understood.
>
> Peter spent the next several hours hanging out at the cabin, alternately feeling worried, hurt, and angry—angry at himself, then at her, then back again at himself. He was already certain that she was The One, his soul mate forever. Why would she push him away like this?
>
> Shannon was not interested in pushing Peter away, nor was she conscious of his hurt feelings that morning. She simply felt like having some time alone. By the time she returned in the late afternoon, Peter had prepared an elaborate feast and had set flowers and candles around the room. Shannon was tickled by the surprise, even if it did seem to be a bit over the top. She gave him a warm kiss and hug, then hastened toward a quick shower before dinner. Peter felt the rush of relief and joy at this reunion, ecstatic again to be so in love with this "amazing" woman.

Peter's emotional roller coaster is being propelled by his internal split. His expectation of rejection leads him to imagine the worst when Shannon elects to hike by herself, leaving him emotionally distraught. His sense of impending tragedy is amplified by his idealized view of her—she is the Goddess, and now he is in danger of losing her. He is compelled to win her back by lavishing attention on her, and becomes ecstatic once more when she accepts his offering.

THE BAD NEWS AND THE GOOD NEWS

Ultimately, the twin branches of the Nice Person's internal split turn out to be two faces of the same coin—the Goddess/Prince Construct (see Chapter Nine, Disillusionment Practice). Each side of the coin is necessitated by the other, and each is inseparable from the other. The entire construct is maintained by the powerful anxiety of the Nice Person. The elevation of idealized lovers (the Pedestal), the sacrifices (the Altar), and the entrapments (the Gilded Cage) are all features that flow from the agitated core of the Nice Person.

The bad news is that Nice People are not likely to change their lives by just trying harder or by memorizing new behavior strategies. The good news is that genuine transformation is indeed possible. It comes from the development of an internal strength and compassion for self which changes the Nice Person from the inside out.

Section Two:
The 7 Practices

Self-help books are like car repair manuals: you can read them all day, but doing so doesn't fix a thing. Working on a car means rolling up your sleeves and getting under the hood, and you have to be willing to get dirt on your hands and grease beneath your fingernails.

—THOMAS LEWIS, MD,
A GENERAL THEORY OF LOVE

As Thomas Lewis suggests in the quote above, it is time to roll up our sleeves and get to work. In this book we provide seven tools (we call them practices since that is what they require) for getting under the hood and fixing the engine. We know that the engine is sputtering with anxious attachment and the valves are clogged with niceness. Now we're going to stick our heads under the hood to get a close look, and start tinkering, tuning, and healing. It is not an accident that we devote four chapters of this book to the problem and eleven chapters to the solution. This is meant to be a dog-eared, grease-stained manual that is eventually tossed in the corner because it isn't needed anymore.

The tools are called the 7 Practices of the Transforming Person. We have already encountered the Nice Person—filled with anxiety and navigating life by trying to please. The Transforming Person uses the 7 Practices to effect a process of continual change and growth in his or her life. Transforming People are living with more conviction and less neediness. They are exercising more compassion and accountability, and less judgment and self-pity. They are becoming calmer and less anxious.

7 PRACTICES OF THE TRANSFORMING PERSON

1. **Awareness Practice**:
   Sustained attention to thoughts, feelings, body, and behavior
2. **Desert Practice**:
   Discovering the source of one's own strength through the practice of solitude (withdrawal from distractions and self-numbing behavior)
3. **Warrior Practice**:
   Taking considered action which integrates both heart and ethic
4. **Brotherhood and Sisterhood Practice**:
   Building same-gender friendships that support transformation
5. **Family Practice**:
   Making sense of childhood and the family experience
6. **Disillusionment Practice**:
   Deconstructing the Prince or Goddess—the illusion of a romantic partner who will magically cure all anxiety, fulfill all dreams, and make life meaningful
7. **Integration Practice**:
   Using daily life as a laboratory for transformation

These practices are a process, not a set of steps. You can do them in any order or at the same time. The practices that you are not "working on" will likely crop up on their own because they are interconnected.

The one practice that is essential to all the others is Awareness Practice. Begin there and continue to keep it in mind as you work with the other practices. From there on, the transformation is highly personal. Perhaps relationships are an immediate issue and Disillusionment Practice is the next place to go. Perhaps the urge for strength and individuation makes Warrior Practice most compelling. Perhaps life has made Desert Practice unavoidable. Or, you may want to work on the practices in the order they are listed.

In the long term, these 7 Practices change the way we think, feel, and act. They can change the shape of our bodies and the shape of our lives. They are well-crafted tools designed for the specific purpose of overcoming chronic anxiety and constructing a life of strength, joy, and extraordinary passion.

Taken all at once, the 7 Practices can feel overwhelming. We advise you begin with Awareness Practice and then pick another practice to work on at the same time

yes yes yes yes yes yes yes yes yes yes yes yes yes yes yes yes yes yes yes yes yes yes yes yes yes yes yes yes yes yes yes yes yes yes
yes yes yes yes yes yes yes yes yes yes yes yes yes yes yes yes yes yes yes yes yes yes yes yes yes yes yes yes yes yes yes yes yes
yes yes yes yes yes yes yes yes yes yes yes yes yes yes yes yes yes yes yes yes yes yes yes yes yes yes yes yes yes yes yes yes yes
yes yes yes yes yes yes yes yes yes yes yes yes yes yes yes yes yes yes yes yes yes yes yes yes yes yes yes yes yes yes yes yes yes
yes yes yes yes yes yes yes yes yes yes yes yes yes yes yes yes yes yes yes yes yes yes yes yes yes yes yes yes yes yes yes yes yes

4

Awareness Practice

Awareness of the present moment is the key.
Practice awareness . . .
Only then will you be free.
Only then will you know abundant joy.

—BUDDHA

Our primary tool for overcoming anxious attachment is Awareness Practice. Put simply, it is sustained attention (sometimes referred to as mindfulness) to thoughts, feelings, body, and behavior. This idea may be familiar to those who have a spiritual or meditative practice. There are any number of well-established methods of practicing awareness, whether it is Zen meditation, Christian contemplation, Sufi dancing, or the communal concentration of the Maple City Knitting Consortium. Each can be a method for being aware of the present moment. The practice we are outlining in this book, however, requires no affiliation, no whirling, not even yarn—just a willingness to become more awake.

Awareness is the practice of bringing sustained attention to thought, emotion, body, and behavior

WHY AWARENESS IS DIFFICULT

Anxiety is experienced as an emotional state, and it can be easy to miss the fact that it is very much a biochemical phenomenon in the body. Many Nice People began absorbing anxiety with their mother's milk and, in some cases, with their food through the umbilicus. This is not mere poetic license. Babies and fetuses affected by the second-hand absorption of these "anxiety chemicals" from their anxious mothers begin to adapt on a cellular level. The more they feel anxiety, the more their bodies acclimate to and prepare for anxiety.

Such early, repeated emotional patterns develop into habitual pathways of thought that go unnoticed by the Nice Person. The mind is affected by these habitual thoughts in the same way that a computer might be affected by a virus. The virus might be performing a host of nefarious and damaging tasks while the user, blithely unaware, continues to work on the computer. This is the way of anxious attachment. It is associated with certain feelings, it inhabits certain cells, it is triggered by certain situations, but it runs its course behind the scenes.

For the Transforming Person, awareness is the foundational step on the path toward receiving love and acceptance. The painful, ironic twist of the Nice Person's existence is that their fear of losing love is the very thing that prevents them from practicing awareness. Nice People believe that if other people see their "weaknesses" they will be rejected. It then becomes of primary importance to the Nice Person to appear happy and helpful, which is a strong incentive to keep their anxious attachment underground. Here is a short list of ways that Nice People suppress the experience of anxiety:

- **The Cloud**: Space out when things are difficult
- **The Drug**: Use caffeine, television, food, shopping, sex, Internet, sugar, alcohol, and (fill in the blank) to stay unaware
- **The Cover Story**: Create an impervious story of your happy, healthy life and stick to it
- **The Armor**: Keep muscles tight to prevent feeling
- **The Sleight of Hand**: Keep constantly preoccupied with solving the problems of others so you can't see your own
- **The Teflon Pan**: Blame difficult feelings on a seemingly unending series of unfortunate external circumstances

As we saw in Chapters One and Two, it is family and society that first create the paths of anxiety in the brain, but it is we ourselves who unconsciously deepen the pathways into ruts. The more often we experience anxiety and consequently develop strategies for avoiding or soothing our anxiety, the deeper the rut gets. Eventually we start channeling any new situation into our anxiety rut. In *A General Theory of Love*, Thomas Lewis says:

The *sine qua non* of a neural network is its penchant for strengthening neuronal patterns in direct proportion to their use. The more often you do or think or imagine a thing, the more probable it is that your mind will revisit its prior stopping point. When the circuits are sufficiently well worn such that thoughts fly down them with little friction or resistance, that mental path has become a part of you—it is now a habit of speech, thought, action, attitude.

Awareness practice is the first step in forging new paths in our brain and new patterns in our heart.

RECOGNIZING NICE PERSON THOUGHTS AND FEELINGS

Our task is to watch the clingy Nice Person thoughts and feelings arise time and time again, bringing them into the light where they will lose their power. Let's look at some Nice Person situations and some corresponding behaviors, emotions, and thoughts.

The Time Accordion

At first you may only notice these thoughts and feelings a week later. "Oh yeah, I did think that. Darn, and I didn't even notice." But with practice you will find yourself noticing a day later and then an hour later, and pretty soon you will notice the thought or feeling as it comes to you.

For some people, feelings precede thoughts. Before a "Nice Person thought" arises, they feel anxious, uncomfortable, evasive, or nervous. Or a

SITUATION	BEHAVIOR	EMOTION	THOUGHT
Nice Guy wants more sex but is afraid to talk to his girlfriend about it.	Nice Guy acts agreeable, as if content	Longing mixed with shame and fear.	"I can't bear how upset she might be if I bring it up."
Nice Girl has a crush on cute young guy at work. Unfortunatley, he flirts with Ms. "Short Skirts" in accounting.	Nice Girl forces conversation, offers to do something for him; watches him when he's not looking; obsesses.	Muted desperation; preoccupied; anxious.	"He ought to be able to see that we're perfect for each other." AND "Rejection is inevitable."
Nice Guy rubbed wife's back last night, stayed up until midnight to fold the laundry because she didn't feel well, and made breakfast for the kids. She's complaining because he had to wake her up to ask where daughter's note for school was.	Nice Guy "forgets" to pick her up from work that afternoon.	Resentment; despair; pride in making sacrifices.	"Of course, if I complain, she'll just say I do all this stuff to buy her love. And then she'll say she wants a real man who can just 'know' what she wants and not have to ask. It's easier to apologize. Maybe later she'll be in a better mood."

person may notice their body's reaction first—tightness in the neck, a hunching of the shoulders, a knot in the stomach, or a clenching of the jaw. Once they pin down the feeling or body awareness, they can set up a kind of alarm system in their head. "I'm feeling anxious, gotta watch out for the Nice

Guy/Nice Girl thoughts!" or "Oh man, my stomach is tense, I wonder if I'm doing Nice Girl/Nice Guy stuff."

When you can actually pay attention to the thoughts that arise, you have reached a crucial moment. Now you have the ability to make a decision—to act differently than you did before. In fact, you may start acting differently even before you're conscious of the choice.

Attending to Words

Words are excellent indicators of thoughts. "I'm sorry," often becomes a Nice Person mantra. It appears to be such an innocent phrase, but often Nice People are not offering a sincere apology; they are apologizing because they feel threatened by the emotional state of the other person. The unbearable feeling inside them comes from their fear of conflict, which might endanger their relationships. When a Nice Person says "I'm sorry," they often mean "Please feel better so that I can feel better."

Another place to be mindful of words is when giving criticism or suggestions to another person. Because conflict frightens Nice People, they often find it impossible to simply state their case. Instead, they cushion their real message with modifying words to soften the blow. Look out for mitigating phrases like: "Maybe it's just me, but" or "This probably isn't a big deal, but" or "I'm probably just confused, but." Observing the words that come after a criticism is also useful. For example, "No big deal really" or "Well, it's just a thought" or "Hey, what do I know?"

Flattery is another red flag. In Chapter Twelve we will discuss the value of a heartfelt compliment, but disingenuous compliments are often a sign of being anxious to please.

NONJUDGMENTAL AWARENESS

Anyone who has meditated can attest that sustaining awareness, though simple, is not easy. A mind might as well be a rhinoceros, charging indiscriminately from one thought to another, unconsciously trampling potentially useful information. Alternatively, a mind is like a tree full of chattering monkeys, one thought vying for attention with the next, shrieking and doing back-flips and throwing banana peels. Sustaining awareness over the din is not easy, but it's doable, and it's life changing.

Practicing nonjudgmental awareness means observing thoughts, feelings, or behaviors without placing a value on them. Before we learn about how to practice nonjudgmental awareness, let's talk about why it is difficult.

Why Nice People Hate Their Niceness

Nice People hate their compulsive niceness for many reasons:
- It causes them to feel:
  - Taken advantage of
  - Looked down on
  - Weak
  - Vulnerable
- It causes damage to:
  - Relationships of all kinds
  - Bodies
  - Careers
  - Spiritual growth

It is painful to notice that our body has chronic ailments, or that we cave in when faced with conflict, or that we have to soothe ourselves with unwanted food, or that we are too frightened to seek a new career, or that we can't confront our spouse. We may even look back over our lifetime and realize how much we have lost or missed out on because we have been anxious to please. We feel shame and guilt and frustration and even more anxiety than we started with.

WARNING:
At first, awareness will intensify the anxiety

On top of that, we notice that we are holding onto years of emotions—unexpressed anger and a constant anxiety—that we have carefully kept hidden. These feelings are exactly the opposite of the stance we have overtly cultivated—Nice People *aren't supposed to be* angry or anxious. This is where judgment comes in. We learned as children that negative emotions don't get us the love we want and therefore we become determined not to have those emotions. When we do have them we label them and ourselves as mean, disgusting, tainted, unlovable, hateful, etc.

Not Judging

Nonjudgmental awareness means that we practice watching our thoughts, feelings, emotions, and body sensations without labeling them as "bad" or "good." The habit of judging ourselves is usually deeply ingrained, largely unconscious, and causes damage in several ways. When we pass judgment on a thought or feeling, we are trying to scare it away so that we can pretend it never existed; lock it away in a compartment where we won't have to examine it; or punish ourselves for having thought or felt it in the first place. But locked away thoughts inevitably escape and scared away thoughts invariably return. The punishment scenario nets us double damage. Not only do we harm ourselves, but usually the thought or feeling that we despise increases in power. It is only by accepting and examining thoughts and feelings that we can discover their source and thus change them.

Judging is a deeply ingrained habit (we even judge our judging!), and it takes practice to be aware of it and then let it go. Imagine a man (who is starting to practice awareness but is still unaware of judging himself), as he wakes up in the morning. He notices that his jaw is tight. He realizes he is tense because he's afraid his wife will be angry with him. Recognizing

Nonjudgmental awareness is at the heart of the Transforming Person

that he has no rational reason to worry that his wife will be angry with him first thing in the morning, he feels embarrassed and starts to mentally berate himself. "I'm such a bastard and I pretend I'm Mr.-Goodie-Two-Shoes. Man, I suck!"

Over time, as we become more adept at recognizing self-judging, it diminishes. But nonjudgment requires a featherlight touch. As a thought or feeling rises up—be it mean or angry or lustful—we can lightly brush it with the feather of awareness. Simply notice the thought or feeling, as "Oh, there's an angry thought," or "That's interesting—I feel annoyed." There is no judging here, just noticing.

Imagine that your awareness is the hand in which you hold your thoughts and emotions. When a thought comes along that you don't like, you are tempted to close your hand into a fist and crush it. But it won't work. When you open your fist the thought will not be gone; it will just take on a different form.

Trying to crush your own thoughts or emotions is the same as trying to crush yourself. This little act of attempted psychic suicide is a message to ourselves that we are unworthy and unloved. If the emotion seems to disappear, it is only an illusion—the emotion has merely disguised itself as something else. We may pretend we don't have anger, but later we will lash out in a passive-aggressive act. We may close our fist on an emotion, but later we may find that it has burrowed into our skin and festered.

So keep the palm open. Observe the emotion or thought without judging it. Allow it to move on when it is done. Acknowledging emotions and thoughts diminishes their power. Awareness practice can take a brewing, unconscious, emotional storm, the kind that might last for weeks and wreak havoc on our emotional landscape, and transform it into a drifting cloud that briefly casts its shadow and is blown away.

Let's take a look at a Nice Person scenario:

Marcia is waiting for a call from her new boyfriend, Don. Because Don was going to the gym after dinner, they agreed he would call her when he got back to his apartment. It's only 9:30 (they didn't set a time) but Marcia is having trouble reading her book. Scenarios keep flickering through her head: What if he got into a car wreck? Or what if he met a woman at the gym? She is alternately worried and angry. By 9:45 she is thinking about how she has told Don of her fear of auto accidents and how she requested that Don help her out by letting her know when he's running late. She begins to feel hurt by his lack of care for her. Marcia grabs a bag of cookies from the kitchen and turns on the television.

Five minutes and five cookies later when Don calls, Marcia has a belly full of anxiety and sugar. Don makes no apologies for the late call and is clearly in good spirits. He asks Marcia how her day went.

Marcia lets him have it. She says that she is sick with worry and she can't understand why he didn't call earlier. Don listens quietly until she asks him if he met another woman at the gym. At that point, Don says he has a busy day tomorrow and abruptly hangs up.

Immediately, Marcia is sick with remorse. "I've done it again," she thinks, "another relationship killed because I flew off the handle. After all, we didn't set a time, and Don is a night owl so he probably thought he was calling early. And he did ask about my day which is incredibly thoughtful."

Marcia digs into the bag of cookies. "Why do I do this over and over? Why can't I just keep my mouth shut! I'm a loser and I'm going to die alone!"

Marcia is terribly anxious and has difficulty with feeling okay about herself when she is involved in a romantic relationship. Perhaps a half hour later, just when Marcia's frustration and self-recrimination reaches a crescendo, she remembers that she was planning on practicing awareness. Take a look at Marcia's awareness practice in the box below.

I'm so stupid! *Okay, wait, I'm really being nasty to myself.* My stomach hurts, I ate all those cookies, stupid, stupid, stupid. *I'm judging again.* Breathe for a second. I'm angry. I just hate when I repeat the same awful mistakes so I eat to make myself feel better which makes me feel worse. *That's a scary thought. True though.* It's this big chain reaction that I set off. So what started it? Why did I say those things to Don? *Good questions.* Because he should have known—wait, no, he really shouldn't have known anything—I didn't tell him what time to call. Ooo, scary, asking for what I want. Could I be any more of a Nice Girl? *More judging.* I just get so nervous. Why? *Good question.* My stomach feels scrunched and I feel all scared and weepy. It's because of the car wreck and...no it really isn't that. How about him meeting another woman, that could happen. Nope. That's not Don. I just get all weird and then I make up these reasons. So the feeling comes first? *That's interesting.* Being alone and away from Don feels really scary to me. What am I afraid of? That he'll leave me. Wow. *That's a breakthrough thought. I think I'm getting better at this!*

Following the thought/feeling/behavior/body trail allows Marcia to work her way down to the heart of the issue. This is a brave act and requires a strong warrior. It is important to point out that there may be more discovery to do here, but Marcia has made a marvelous start. She is practicing several important things:

- Breaking her cycle of self-punishment and misery
- Moving through painful thoughts and emotions more quickly by observing them dispassionately
- Turning unspecified, frightening thoughts and emotions into specific, manageable thoughts and emotions
- Uncovering useful revelations
- Giving herself the opportunity to act from a position of strength and clarity

The last may seem surprising. Why would it be a position of strength to acknowledge that you get anxious and weepy when your boyfriend doesn't call? Because knowledge gives birth to choice and choice leads to change. For instance, Marcia may wish to call Don and apologize. Perhaps they have already discussed her transformational practices or, if not, maybe this is the time for her to tell him. Hopefully, Don will be frank with her, perhaps letting her know that he felt offended by her intimations. He may even tell her that he appreciates her courage and honesty. They may want to work on a solution (such as Marcia asking Don to call by a certain time if that is what she needs). And, of course, the entire telephone conversation is another opportunity for Marcia to practice awareness.

Knowledge gives birth to choice, and choice leads to change

Now, what would have happened if Marcia had reminded herself to practice awareness before Don called? Well, she might have already recognized the anxious feeling in her tummy, and her warning signals might have gone up. "Nice Girl alert!" She might not have grabbed the cookies, or she might have grabbed them, realized she wasn't hungry, decided to just eat two, and then put them away. Maybe when Don called, the first thing she would have said is, "Don, I'm really glad you called. I'm feeling pretty upset. Can I talk to you about it?" Marcia, the Transforming Woman, is practicing awareness and handling her relationship in a very different way than she is used to. This simple act of noticing is powerful and can change the course of Marcia's lifelong cycle of broken relationships.

GRACE

Grace is an essential component of nonjudgmental awareness. By grace we mean the actions and attitudes that arise in a Transforming Person when they have developed compassion for themselves. This can take many forms:

- Developing patience for watching repetitive thoughts or harmful behavior
- Forgiving yourself for making mistakes
- Forgiving the child you were
- Learning to pat yourself on the back for having the courage to look at difficult or frightening emotions, thoughts, or behavior
- Having a sense of humor (perhaps the most important grace)

All of this is about recognizing that we are human beings and that each of us plays the fool from time to time. It is a startling irony that our darkness (our negative thoughts and feelings) is the portal to change. So when the Nice Person behavior seems most acute or stubborn or painful, it is often a sign that deep down, change is happening. Remember that we are doing difficult work—work which most people are afraid to attempt. We are Transforming People, not transformed people. We are worthy of compassion. We are worthy of a good laugh. We are worthy of grace.

Self-Indulgence

For the Nice Person, compassion can be a walk on the razor's edge. On the one side of the razor is self-flagellation (judging, demeaning, and dismissing the self), and on the other side is self-indulgence. Nice People are prone to self-indulgence because (1) they want their anxiety to go away, and (2) they have made a habit of not taking care of themselves. When they want to be soothed, or be medicated, or to check out, they have no internal model for restraint. "I've had a long day, and I just want (some M&Ms?, to skip the gym?, to buy another pair of shoes?, etc.)." None of these indulgencies are necessarily bad things to do or have. It's the motivation that counts. The Nice Person often wants to indulge in order to forget their anxiety. Like putting whiskey in the baby bottle so the kid will stop crying, self-indulgence is ultimately neglectful. The antidote to self-indulgence is a mature and fierce warrior which we will explore in Chapter Six.

THE CYCLE OF AWARENESS

The cyclic model shows how awareness builds on itself. It is tempting to think of awareness as being like a door that we have to get through. But the door metaphor is inadequate because it implies a process with a distinct ending: "Once I find the key, I'm set!" The exciting thing about the cyclic model of awareness is that it provides ongoing revelation and results. Look at the diagram on page 71.

THE CYCLE OF AWARENESS

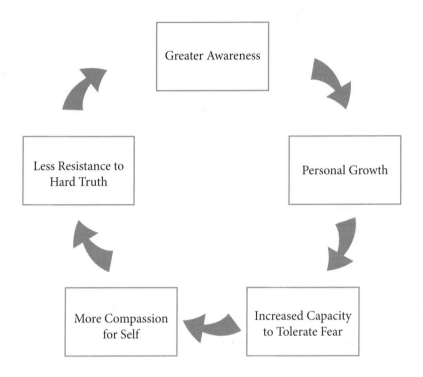

Now consider the example of Jack who makes a discovery about himself:

In my family, sexuality was hush-hush—it was never discussed or acknowledged. That's why I still get tense about sex and I avoid sexual situations.

There is a sense of release in a new thought of this kind because it has been a closely held secret which Jack no longer has to carry around. He relaxes incrementally, and perhaps he is able to discuss the issue with a trusted friend. Personal growth occurs as Jack allows this new knowledge to settle in. He may still be nervous about sexual situations, but he is no longer frightened of what is hidden in his subconscious and that is a great relief. Best of all, Jack increases his capacity for tolerating fear by repeatedly looking it squarely in the face and discovering that he is still okay.

Once Jack is able to look at his fear, compassion for himself becomes easier. He realizes that as a child he could not possibly have understood all the unspoken tension in his household. He realizes that he probably did the smartest and safest thing he could do as a kid in that circumstance—he didn't bring up the subject of sex and tried hard not to think about it. Now Jack is developing compassion not only with the child he was, but with the person he has become. He feels grief at the knowledge that he carried such anxiety about sex for so many years. Jack begins to let go of his anxiety. He finds that his body feels a bit different—lighter and looser. Over time, Jack's brain equates awareness with feeling better, and he learns to welcome hard truth.

The Healing Helix

Because Transforming People come back again and again to subtle variations of the same Nice Guy/Nice Girl problems, it can sometimes seem like they're getting nowhere. The cycle of awareness can sometimes feel more like a hamster's treadmill on which the Nice Person scurries endlessly. There are several remedies for this feeling. One is to take a step back and look at your progress.

> Bob goes to a new car dealer in the morning having already picked out the car, the options, and the price he wants. Three hours later, he barely escapes from a team of hard-sell experts who are intent on selling him a car he doesn't want. He didn't stand his ground or get his car or even give them a piece of his mind. "Nice Guy Bob" strikes again!
>
> It's time for Bob to take a look at his progress. For the last five years Bob has been driving a car he hates because he couldn't bring himself to confront the last car dealer who bullied him into buying it. This time, rather than caving in and buying car he didn't want, he simply walked out. Sure, Bob's still facing the same Nice Person problem, but he is facing it with a completely different level of skillfulness.

It may be useful to think of the cycle of awareness as a spiral or helix. We may return to the same point relative to the core (the core being our most basic personality traits), but each time around, as we become more aware and handle things with more skillfulness, we find ourselves higher up on the helix.

VIGILANCE

Nice Person thoughts have two things in common with horror movies:

- Nice Person emotions and thoughts keep coming back from the dead.
- Nice Person emotions and thoughts can be transformed by exposure to light.

Again and again we watch the anxiety in our body, brain, and heart arise. And like the brave heroine or hero in the movie, a Transforming Person must remain vigilant. The bright light of our awareness is the daylight that monsters cannot abide—it saps their power to control our behavior, and over time, they become less powerful. Eventually, we are able to easily recognize a Nice Person feeling at the moment it arises. "Oh, hello, are you still hanging around? You're that old 'I'm-afraid-to-say-*no*-because-they-won't-love-me,' emotion. Well come on in, sit down, have a cup of coffee." No longer cloaked in the frightening shadows of the subconscious, the emotion no longer seems quite as monstrous.

Awareness requires vigilance

ALL ROADS LEAD TO ROME

Awareness practice is the fundamental tool for transforming anxiety into serenity and timidity into courage. It can be practiced anywhere at any time. It does not require an appointment or equipment or joining a league because what Nice People are observing are themselves and their anxious attachment. Do you find yourself getting angry when you drive? Do you have trouble experiencing joy when something goes your way? Does the idea of conflict at work make your stomach hurt? Do you snap at your partner when you don't mean to? Do you pick at them in your head? Have you carried tension in your body so long that you no longer notice it?

Every thought, feeling, body function, and behavior is a legitimate subject for awareness. Transforming People can choose to be aware at any time, and if they apply compassion, grace, and vigilance, marvelous changes will take place.

Activities That Support Awareness Practice

Obviously any activity can promote awareness, but some are specifically designed for the task. Among them we recommend:

- Meditation (meditation is a concentrated form of awareness practice)
- Psychotherapy (a good psychotherapist provides both a safe, contained environment for awareness practice, and a neutral mirror to allow for reflection)
- Healing arts (acupuncture, massage, etc., provide an opportunity to learn where anxiety is stuck and how it moves through your body)
- Men's/women's groups, twelve-step groups, etc. (can provide many of the same benefits as psychotherapy in an environment of fellowship)
- Brotherhood and Sisterhood (allows for encouragement, support, and honest reflection)
- Journaling (writing incites awareness and is an excellent tool for shaping and crystallizing ideas)
- Martial arts (any practice that sharpens the mind and body improves awareness practice)

A list of the activities that *inhibit* awareness practice would be longer than this chapter. Anything that Nice People do to cloud their mind, bury their emotions, deaden their bodies, or ignore their behavior, makes awareness practice more difficult. Many activities can be employed to heighten awareness *or* obscure it, depending on a person's intentions. Sex, food, exercise, conversation—all can be enlightening, enervating, or anything in between.

COMPASSION FOR SELF

It is worth emphasizing the indispensability of grace. Nice People will face their anxiety again and again. Just when they think they've got it licked they will pull the same Nice Person stunt and then have to battle adding insult to injury through self-recrimination and guilt. These corrosive patterns are tenacious, so it is essential that the Transforming Person develop persistence in their own compassion. The fellowship of loving friends will become invaluable in supporting this vigilant compassion.

What the Nice Person needs to understand is that they have a lifetime pattern of minimizing their "niceness," of brushing it off, and protesting to themselves that it really shouldn't be such a big deal. But their anxiety was imprinted in their hearts at a time when getting mommy's love was a matter of life and death. It *is* a big deal.

Nice People must acknowledge that they are doing important, difficult work. They are modern heroic knights, and the slippery, difficult-to-touch anxiety of their childhood is the dragon. They do not seek to slay this dragon, but rather to transform it with compassion.

Remember:
- You are doing difficult work.
- Give yourself comfort and encouragement.
- Bravery is choosing to get back up and try again.

PACKING FOR THE DESERT

It is an equally marvelous and frustrating mystery that the very things Nice People do that make awareness practice difficult (remember the Cloud, the Drug, the Cover Story, the Armor, the Sleight of Hand, and the Teflon Pan?) are precisely the things on which they must focus their awareness. In that paradox lies the secret to transformation.

Nice People deeply long for serenity. To find it they must work with their anxiety. They wish for light and must seek it in their darkness. They thirst for clean, cool water and must seek it in the desert. Such riddles are frustrating and difficult to understand until they are experienced.

Chapter Five is Desert Practice. Pack lightly. Yourself, your awareness, and your compassion are all that will be required.

yes yes

5

Desert Practice

Face your deficiencies and acknowledge them; but do not let them master you. Let them teach you patience, sweetness, insight. When we do the best we can, we never know what miracle is wrought in our life, or in the life of another.

—HELEN KELLER

We are not afraid to follow truth wherever it may lead.

—THOMAS JEFFERSON

THIS IS THE LAND OF CONFUSION

As we practice awareness, it becomes increasingly apparent that there are many factors making it difficult to notice thoughts, feelings, body sensations, and behavior. These distracting or numbing elements are not there by accident—many of them were created for the specific purpose of blocking the painful feelings coming from anxious attachment. Nice People have been unconsciously creating roadblocks to awareness their whole lives, setting up chaotic circumstances, mental detours, and emotional misdirection. They might become obsessed with work or a relationship, overindulge in food, or numb themselves with drugs or alcohol.

Desert Practice is the conscious act of withdrawing from distracting and numbing elements for the purpose of more directly experiencing oneself. This practice involves encountering painful emotions that have long been avoided, but it also involves the discovery of resources that have been lost. More importantly, it forms the basis for a new relationship with the self, ultimately leading to an abiding sense of acceptance.

From time immemorial there have been stories of people who go through a period of retreat before emerging, transformed, to face the great challenges of their lives with newfound strength and resolve. Passing through such a period requires great courage and persistence, and seems to always involve confrontation of one's deepest fears. Desert Practice is an indispensable component in the transformation from being chronically nice to living a life of strength, kindness, and extraordinary passion. The Desert is not simply a phase, but is an ongoing practice to which the Transforming Person returns as needed.

> **Desert Practice is the conscious act of withdrawing from distracting and numbing elements for the purpose of more directly experiencing oneself**

Trips to the Desert are often driven by desperation. A significant loss or major shift in the conditions of life can require us to undergo a profound change in order to survive and eventually thrive. But even though life circumstances may *drive* us into the Desert, we may also *choose* to go there in order to grow and reflect.

EMOTIONAL CHALLENGES OF DESERT PRACTICE

In the quieter space of the Desert, we can study and work with painful and challenging emotions, promoting a host of benefits (see below). Even so, the intensity of these feelings can be disturbing, and it may be helpful to know that they are to be expected. Common experiences in the Desert include:

- Grief and rage from losses related to a lifetime of anxious attachment
- Fear of uncovering unhealthy Nice Person behavior

- Despair about repetition of Nice Person patterns
- Escalation of anxiety from withdrawal from distracting and numbing elements

BENEFITS OF DESERT PRACTICE

The Desert is a place that is designed to promote healing, and there are many wonderful things to be gained for the person who is willing to undergo the challenges of this practice. These benefits include:

- Deep acceptance of self
- Pleasure in caring for self
- Increased contentment
- Enjoyment of your own company
- Ownership of sexual fulfillment
- Celebration of your own masculinity or femininity

BASICS OF DESERT PRACTICE

At its most elemental, Desert Practice is an act of doing without something (or someone) for the purpose of generating reflection, insight, and strength. Throughout history this process has taken a myriad of different forms. Even so, each form tends to have at least these three elements:

1. A Starting Point: a person, place, thing, or behavior from which to abstain or withdraw
2. A Structure
3. A Practice of Awareness

Element #1: The Starting Point

It should be noted that the person doing the Desert Practice doesn't always get to choose the starting point. Often, a time in the Desert begins with an unplanned circumstance, such as the loss of a relationship, job, home, etc. When you choose to use the occasion as an opportunity for growth and reflection, you are doing Desert Practice.

Element #2: The Structure

The structure gives parameters for the time in the Desert, providing safety and support to optimize the work. The structure might include such things as:

- **Physical space:** Where you are can have a big impact on your ability to reflect. Be as conscious and intentional as you can be about choosing physical surroundings to minimize intrusion and maximize reflection.
- **Company:** Even if you are withdrawing from a relationship, be aware of the people around you and choose people who will support the purpose of your Desert time.
- **An "*Until…*" clause:** Setting a time limit allows you to know that this won't go on indefinitely while bringing clarity to your purpose (e.g., "…for one week" or "…until I am sleeping through the night").

Element #3: The Practice of Awareness

The feelings and thoughts that are evoked during Desert Practice are like ore that has been excavated from the earth: in raw form, they are not nearly as useful as when they have been processed and refined. Insight develops out of awareness, and with insight comes an increased ability to make long-lasting changes.

A boat sitting in its usual liquid habitat is always partially obscured, with large portions of it remaining unseen below the water line. Sometimes the owner will bring it in to a dry dock where the boat is raised up out of the water and suspended on land so that inspections and repairs can be made on the lower portions of the vessel that normally remain unseen. Nice People also have parts that live below the water line—feelings, thoughts, and behaviors that usually remain outside of awareness. The ability to examine these things is often obscured by a sea of distractions and numbing agents. Desert Practice is a kind of dry dock where the Transforming Person can pull out of the elements of their usual life in order to examine themselves more carefully and clearly.

SPECIFIC HABITS OF DESERT PRACTICE

What follows are several habits that can be of great use to Transforming People as they walk through the Desert. Each person has unique needs and challenges, and you may find some of these habits to be simple while others seem nigh unto impossible. Pay special attention to the impossible ones; there is probably something important there for you.

Habit: Solitude

The choice of taking time alone has been a feature of many spiritual and healing practices, and it has particular significance for Transforming People. Those who are coping with anxious attachment are fearful of being abandoned and neglected. They will habitually sacrifice their time, energy, and self-esteem to ensure that they are not alone. As a result, they often find themselves in relationships that are not good for them, playing out roles that harm them even though they never really find the security that they seek.

For this reason, the choice to spend time alone is an essential (and often scary) activity for Transforming People. Being alone evokes symptoms of anxious attachment. If done with care and compassion, it can create a good laboratory for studying and transforming emotions, thoughts, body sensations, and behaviors.

Being alone also creates space to reflect on the relationships in your life (note that this is different from taking a sabbatical from romance and/or sex, which is discussed below). It can be hard to think about the dynamics of a relationship when the other person is sitting right next to you. Sometimes a different perspective can be found with just a few minutes of separation; at other times, it may take days or weeks apart to be able to sort out the complicated threads of a relationship.

As we practice solitude it becomes apparent that we are anxious and needy *whether or not* the other person is around. This awareness eventually offsets the tendency to cling because (1) we are more conscious of the clinging impulse and (2) we recognize that the other person is not the answer to our need, no matter how loving and helpful they might be.

One of the greatest benefits of taking time alone is the development of the "aloneness muscle." If solitude is practiced with compassion and moderation, you will become more and more comfortable with being alone and with experiencing your own separateness. The emphasis on "moderation" here is important—going too far outside of your comfort zone can have the effect of increasing the sense of fear and panic, at least in the short term.

It is not enough, however, to experience separateness from others. The crucial piece has to do with experiencing yourself. The point is not simply to be alone, but to be alone with *you*—getting to know yourself, befriending yourself, and learning to recognize your own voice.

This can be a highly erratic and frustrating endeavor. You may not know what your inner voice sounds like. Your inner voice may seem to go completely silent on you, or it may seem to be chattering in your ears constantly, urging conflicting or chaotic thoughts. The encounter with yourself is where compassion becomes of the highest importance. The challenge is to practice the kind of love and acceptance toward yourself that a good parent offers their new child: unconditional, no matter what you find, to the utmost of your ability. This love is the most powerful agent of transformation that you have, and is the element that makes solitude really pay off.

TIPS FOR PRACTICING SOLITUDE

Choose the best challenge level for yourself. If being alone is hard for you, create a structure that is challenging enough to get your juices going but not so much that you are overwhelmed.

Get support. Consult friends and others (like a therapist or spiritual guide) and arrange to have these people available for talking about your experiences.

Be intentional about the structure. Different people need different kinds of solitude. For some, a few hours alone on a walk pushes the limits; for others, a two-week backpack trip in the mountains is just the ticket.

Regular practice. Make solitude a consistent part of your life, not just something you do once or twice. Part of the idea is to become comfortable with being aware of your own thoughts and experiencing things by yourself.

Practice loving what you're doing. Do something you love when you're alone. Lean into your enjoyment of it. Whenever possible, savor the joy of having you to yourself.

Accept your anxiousness. Practicing solitude can evoke intense anxiety, and it can help to know this ahead of time. By choosing an appropriate challenge level for yourself, you can discover that the anxiety is bearable. Eventually, you come to an acceptance of the anxiety, which paradoxically brings more calmness and confidence.

Practice recognizing your own accomplishment. If you've done something that was difficult in service of your own growth, it's important to take a moment to recognize this. Avoid comparisons to what you think other people can do—each of us has our own unique path, and you are the one who can best understand what represents an act of courage and commitment to self.

Habit: Fashioning Your Own Life

If a thing is worth doing, it's worth doing poorly.
—ATTRIBUTED TO G.K. CHESTERTON

The development of an aesthetic may seem to be far down the list of important skills for the Transforming Person, but for some it may be the most difficult and fruitful element of Desert Practice. This is not about becoming stylish or impressing others with your fashion sense; it is about learning to listen to that little voice inside that actually has an opinion.

Nice People focus a lot of their attention on sensing what other people want, and subsequently remain unaware of what they want for themselves.

They are more likely to know what styles are accepted or preferred by others than they do about what aesthetic particularly calls to them, and sometimes they have no sense of it whatsoever.

Each Nice Person has his or her own strengths and weaknesses, of course, and some do have a clear idea of how they prefer things to look and feel. Even so, it is common (especially among Nice Guys) to feel completely at sea when it comes to decorating or shopping for clothes. For these Nice People, torture is having the job of outfitting the new apartment.

This means that the process of developing an aesthetic is an act of courage for the transforming Nice Person. Simply choosing a paint color or picking out a new outfit may represent a big step forward for some, whereas remodeling a kitchen is a good challenge for others.

TIPS FOR FASHIONING YOUR LIFE

Start where you are. If you don't have much experience exercising your own aesthetic, start with something small. Go buy yourself one new blouse or pair of shoes, or choose one new item for your bedroom or living room.

Consultation is okay, but make sure you're in charge. There's nothing wrong with asking for input from friends and partners, but it's important that you feel in charge of the process. Form your own opinion *before* asking anyone else for theirs. Or, see how it feels to make your choices without seeking any opinions at all.

Experiment. Approach each step as one in a series of experiments. You cannot develop your aesthetic by deduction—you have to try a lot of things that don't work before discovering what's just right for you.

Follow your bliss. Pay attention to what calls to you, interests you, or tickles your fancy, then stretch yourself by taking it a little bit further. If you find that you like the color mauve, paint a wall or try on some clothes with that color.

Habit: Developing Better Same-Gender Relationships

One of the most important resources for sustaining a Transforming Person is a network of same-gender friends. We refer to these networks as the Brotherhood and Sisterhood. Chapter Seven is devoted entirely to this topic, but it is worth emphasizing a few points right now about this important habit.

As we have noted, the Desert can be a lonely place, eliciting deeply painful emotions—feeling literally deserted. We will instinctively seek some form of solace from these feelings, and our instincts will often lead us in directions that are not particularly good for us. Healthy and supportive friendships provide a vital sustenance that helps us to make conscious choices about addressing our own needs.

Platonic same-gender friends can provide a quality of feedback, understanding, and communion that is not attainable in other relationships. These relationships are uncluttered by gender differences or romantic interests, and are rooted in common experiences of being female or male. Recent research has enhanced our understanding of neurological, hormonal, emotional, and behavioral differences between women and men, bringing empirical support to the notion that a unique understanding is possible within same-gender friendships. For the Transforming Person, that unique understanding can be invaluable.

Habit: Taking a Sabbatical from Romance and Sex

The term "sabbatical" shares a linguistic root with "Sabbath" and refers to a time that is set aside for reflection and rejuvenation. It is a period of taking a break from a life-as-usual pattern in order to take stock of behaviors and priorities.

Taking a sabbatical from romantic and/or sexual matters can be structured in a variety of ways, depending on the needs of the Transforming Person. These might include taking a break from:

- Dating
- Dating websites, personal ads
- Sex with yourself (masturbation)
- Sex with someone else

- Any form of erotica or pornography
- Romance novels or romantic movies

For most people, taking a break from just one thing (e.g., dating) will be quite enough to stir things up. Add any other romantic or sexual behaviors that you think should also be included in the list above. As you look at each item, imagine what it would be like to stop that behavior. Pay close attention to any behaviors that have an emotional charge or urgency attached to them. These are the behaviors to consider for the sabbatical.

When setting up the structure for your sabbatical, choose an "*Until…*" clause—in other words, choose a specific limit for how long you'll do this. For example:

- "I will give up reading romance novels until I have a clear understanding of how they affect my view of relationships."
- "I'm going to stop masturbating until June 15th."
- "I'm going to refrain from dating for six months."

Keep in mind that the purpose of the sabbatical is to give yourself a temporary sanctuary for reflecting on the meanings and experiences of sex and romance in your life. It is of utmost importance that this process be one of loving restraint and not a subtle form of self-abuse or deprivation. The practice of nonjudgmental awareness is the most powerful way to keep your sabbatical healthy.

While the romance/sex sabbatical may seem similar to the solitude habit talked about earlier, its purpose and structure are different. The solitude habit is about creating time alone in order to discover yourself and to hear your own voice; the romance/sex sabbatical is about examining the ways that the powerful dynamics of sex and romance play out in your life and your psyche.

SABBATICALS AND SIGNIFICANT OTHERS

A romance/sex sabbatical can have an important impact on a significant other, whether that person is a spouse of fifty years or someone you've been dating for a few months. If you have a relationship that will be affected by your sabbatical, keep a few things in mind:

- **Discuss your plans ahead of time.** Let your partner know what you're planning to do and why you're doing it. Your sabbatical will go better if your partner knows what's coming, particularly if he or she is willing to support your plan.
- **Be willing to negotiate the details without giving up the purpose.** If you're taking a break from something that affects your partner, it is important to listen to how they feel about that and to have some willingness to modify your structure in order to make it work for them. The challenge is to be open to their needs while being vigilant about any tendencies to be overly accommodating.
- **Don't take a long break from affection.** If your sabbatical involves stopping physical or romantic intimacy that is a healthy component of your relationship, don't make it a long break. Take as long as you need to be able to feel the absence and to study its affects on you.
- **Watch out for passive-aggression.** Nice People are particularly prone to being passive-aggressive. Examine your own motives to be sure that your abstention is in service of your own growth and not a form of withholding from your partner.

Habit: Learning to Care for Yourself

As we said at the beginning of the chapter, Desert Practice is about developing the capacity to care for yourself. It is not about being a loner or denying the need to rely on others, but about finding a wonderful source of water within yourself. For Transforming People this is an essential shift in orientation, one that involves letting go of the hope that someone else will be responsible for taking care of us or making life worth living.

It is an important part of Desert Practice, then, to develop specific habits of self-care. This can be a major challenge for Nice People who have accepted long ago that a state of neediness is the usual state of affairs. When beginning these new habits, Transforming People often feel as though they are pampering or indulging themselves; in fact, they are finally caring for themselves for the first time.

Imagine that you are a baby and are utterly helpless. All day long you need things—food, affection, stimulation, comfort, sleep, and so on. You have only the tool of vocalization (i.e., crying, cooing, etc.) to get someone's attention; after that, you are totally dependent upon your caregiver's providence.

Now, consider the fact that in your current adult form you have virtually every need that you had as a baby (food, affection, etc.). The primary difference is that you now have all of the skills that the caregiver should have, *and* you have one more asset that Mom, Dad, and the babysitter lacked: you already know exactly what you're experiencing. If you're thirsty, you can tell whether you need a lot or a little, whether it's water, Gatorade, or iced tea that will best quench your thirst. You can think about nuances, like what your current caloric needs are or whether your blood sugar needs a boost. You are the world's leading expert on the subject of you.

Learning to care for oneself is a life-long process that requires occasional updating and retooling. What you needed five years ago may not quite fit what you need to today, which may be different from what you will need five years from now.

As you learn to practice self-care, being out of balance will not feel as normal or acceptable as it once did. You will become accustomed to the regular experience of a calm healthiness in body, mind, and spirit.

TIPS FOR PRACTICING SELF-CARE

- **Care for what goes into your body.** Choosing the foods that are good for you, eating the right amounts, drinking enough water; monitoring intake of caffeine, sugar, and fat; examining use of altering substances (alcohol, marijuana, tobacco, etc.).
- **Care for how you use your body.** Getting enough exercise, getting the right kinds of exercise for your body, monitoring stress, getting sufficient rest and sleep.

- **Receive care for your body**, such as massage, acupuncture, physical affection (sexual and nonsexual touch), and regular physical exams.
- **Care for your emotional and psychological needs**: reserve time for yourself, invest in caring and healthy relationships; psychotherapy; follow a spiritual path or practice; meditate; keep a journal.

LEAVING THE DESERT

The Desert is a place of retreat, contemplation, and repair for the Transforming Person, and each time we go there we become more competent in its practices. When the time is right, we will return to the more familiar confines of regular life, bringing with us new-found resources that will feed our minds, hearts, and relationships. The raw material that has been mined in the Desert is now ready to be integrated into a new level of being: the Warrior.

6

Warrior Practice

The path of the Warrior is lifelong,
and mastery is often simply staying on the path.
—RICHARD STROZZI HECKLER,
IN SEARCH OF THE WARRIOR SPIRIT

WHAT WE MEAN BY "WARRIOR"

A "warrior," in the way we use the term, is a woman or man who has a conscious personal ethic, who is able to hold intense emotions, and who takes considered action that follows both their heart and ethic. In the tradition of Eastern martial arts we believe that a warrior brings a set of skills to whatever conflict he or she faces. Our warrior is facing, first and foremost, an internal struggle—wrestling with his or her own demons to achieve mastery of the self. In the first several chapters of this book we described the demons that plague Nice People, and clearly they are powerful and numerous. It requires courage, strength, and persistence—attributes of the warrior—to grapple with these most basic fears and desires.

THE THREE DIMENSIONS OF THE WARRIOR

Warrior Practice is action that flows from a conscious personal ethic and an ability to hold strong emotions.

THREE DIMENSIONS OF THE WARRIOR

1. A personal ethic: values formed from conscious reflection
2. A growing ability to tolerate intense emotion without reflexive action
3. A practice of taking action which follows both heart and ethic

---

1. A Personal Ethic

"What do I believe? What are my values? How should I live?" These are questions that Nice People avoid when the answers conflict with their habit of accommodating the needs of others. The good news is that once a Transforming Person starts practicing awareness, they are already well on their way to a personal ethic because a central element in developing an ethos is the willingness to examine their own behavior.

Warrior Practice is about conviction, whether in taking action or in the decision not to take action. The warrior's conviction comes from having a *conscious personal* ethic.

When a Nice Person is presented with a decision, they often find it very difficult to act with conviction. Either they react emotionally (out of fear or anger or neediness), or they act from an impersonal ethic—expressing the values of a religion, special interest group, teacher, or the culture at large. There is nothing wrong with having the same values as others, but to become a warrior requires a *personal* ethic. That means that the values have been tested against body, heart, and mind, and found compatible.

Our lives present us with an ongoing personal ethics workshop. Any situation that requires a person to make a decision will do. A Nice Person, in any given situation, will likely acquiesce to someone else's wishes, not because they think it is the right thing to do, but because they have anxiety about causing conflict or losing friendship, love, or status. They will then find ways to sublimate the uncomfortable feelings that will likely accompany their decision. The Transforming Person in the same situation will look inside themselves and ask, "What is right for me?" This is the question of a warrior.

A simple action can be either the compulsive gesture of a Nice Person or the mature ethical stance of a warrior. For instance, a person encountering a beggar on the street has many options:

ACTION	NICE PERSON THOUGHTS	WARRIOR THOUGHTS
Give the beggar $10 and keep walking.	If I throw a big bill he'll thank me and everyone at the bus stop will know what a generous person I am.	I believe in helping a person where I find them. I'm doing well financially, and I've got extra money this week.
Give the beggar your spare change and keep walking.	I don't feel like giving this beggar money but I don't want a confrontation.	I've decided I can afford to give my change to one person a day. I know this guy by sight and we're both part of the same neighborhood.
Give the beggar some money and stop for a chat.	I want to help this guy, but he might think I'm a jerk if I just throw money at him.	If I'm going to give someone money I believe that I should get to know them. Sometimes, showing some interest can mean as much as the cash.

Understand that a warrior may also feel uncomfortable. But in one case, actions are driven by anxious thoughts and feelings; in the other, actions are driven by a personal ethic.

2. Tolerating Intense Emotion without Reflexive Action

Nice People have highly sensitive defense mechanisms, particularly when they are being confronted with the idea that they have not been considerate or that they have acted badly. These feel like attacks on the central character points (i.e., their "niceness") that they believe make them lovable, the character points that they developed in childhood to survive. Once a sore point has been engaged, the reaction is swift and harsh. It may be to give up, confess, and weep, or it may be to get belligerent and snipe from behind cover, or it may be to put up an impenetrable shield and hide. Whatever the mechanism, it was developed long ago, and now happens without the person thinking about it.

REEDUCATING THE REFLEXES

The question is: How do we slow down or stop this seemingly automatic reflexive action? Let's take another look at the cycle of awareness.

This time, we're entering the cycle at "Increased Capacity to Tolerate Emotion" because reflexive reaction is caused when a situation engages the basic fears of the anxiously attached.

Three steps to increasing the capacity to tolerate intense emotion are:

1. Becoming aware of the emotion
2. Examining the emotion
3. Developing compassion for the emotion

As we have seen, these three steps are difficult because Nice People have an enormous investment in hiding or ignoring their emotions. But a warrior is willing to practice awareness even though their Nice Person reflexes are telling them that it is dangerous, and their Nice Person brain is wondering if they wouldn't rather have a sandwich and watch a sitcom. And even if the Transforming Person does eat that sandwich and watch that sitcom, the

CYCLE OF AWARENESS

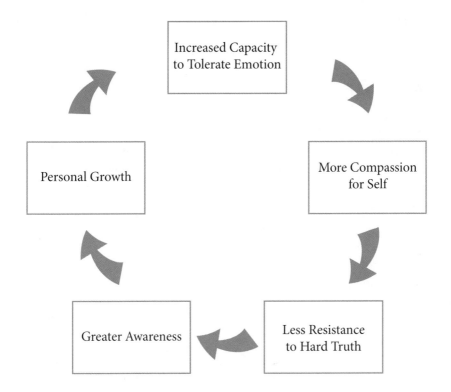

warrior in them says, "Stay aware. This sandwich and this TV show are clues. There is something here I need to pay attention to."

Once the Nice Person thought is hunted down, it takes a warrior to drag it into the light and examine it. There may be embarrassment and hurt feelings, but the warrior is tenacious and will not be denied.

The last step, compassion, more than anything else, requires a warrior's strength. These two words, "compassion" and "warrior," are two sides of the same coin, and from them emanates a ferocious heart. It takes a warrior to thwart a lifetime of judgment and condemnation and say, "I see my jealousy

A warrior fosters a ferocious heart

and it is harmful and I don't like it. I accept it as mine and will not condemn myself for what I feel. I understand how I came to it. I love myself and wish for this emotion to diminish, and in the meantime I will be careful that I do not hurt anyone else."

SPACIOUSNESS

Practicing the tolerance of intense emotions requires the proper internal space. Imagine designing a container for a headstrong colt. You probably want a good-sized corral so the colt is free to run and kick up its legs without getting hurt. But you have to have a solid fence or the colt is liable to break out and leave the safety of the corral. This is the same feeling we need inside ourselves: plenty of room for our emotions to run their course, but with a good solid container so that they do not overwhelm us or harm us. It requires a warrior to build and maintain this space.

No matter how tough and successful our warrior is, some emotions still hurt. But once we have developed this internal sense of spaciousness, we no longer have to fear being overwhelmed.

3. Taking Action

The first two dimensions of the warrior bring depth (personal ethic) and breadth (capacity for tolerating intense emotion), aligning the head and the heart. The third dimension of the warrior, then, is about taking action that flows from this internal foundation. Here's an example:

> Lewis is a former Nice Guy who is the business director for an art museum. He works on equal footing with the founder of the museum who is also the chief curator. Recently, they have been disagreeing over the next year's budget. Things have been looking up lately, and Lewis proposed a conservative increase in the budget from $1.4 million to $1.6 million in order to take advantage of the recent growth. The chief curator says that he has a chance to land two opportunity-of-a-lifetime

exhibits and that the budget must be increased to $2 million to accommodate these rare finds. The chief curator is wildly excited and he has prepared a document showing that if every grant comes through, and every donor donates the maximum, and every exhibit is a big hit, the museum will be able to sustain a $2 million budget. Lewis points out that no business counts on everything coming through. He counters with $1.7 million, suggesting that the chief curator choose one of his two new projects. Though this figure is at the very limit of the museum's fundraising capacity, Lewis thinks it might be obtainable. Eventually, the chief curator agrees. One week later, Lewis receives an email from the chief curator addressed to both himself and the museum's board of directors stating that the next year's budget will be $1.9 million and announcing the two new projects.

Lewis sits down and writes a scalding reply to the chief curator and the entire board. He not only points out the underhanded nature of this particular situation, but goes into the chief curator's past history of selfish and childish behavior that has endangered the entire organization. For good measure he suggests that one of the chief curator's pet projects was chosen to further his personal résumé and is a poor choice for the museum. Lewis grabs the mouse and moves the cursor to the send button.

But as Lewis scans his words a last time, his Awareness Practice kicks in. He realizes his chest is tight and that he can barely breathe. This is a Nice Guy alarm for Lewis. He decides not to send the email just yet. He lets go of the mouse and checks in with himself. He is intensely angry but feels that the situation clearly warrants his anger. However, as Lewis monitors his anger he realizes it is not just directed at the chief curator. Lewis has been in this position over and over in various arts organizations, being pushed around and undermined, and every time he has backed down and ultimately accepted responsibility for other people's bad decisions in order to save the organization from looking bad. In each instance, the organization has floundered trying to meet impossible expectations, and Lewis himself has been overwhelmed with the burden of trying to meet an unrealistic budget. Now, looking at his personal attack on the chief curator, Lewis admits that he is trying to make up for all the times he has allowed himself to be pushed around. Lewis realizes that he is also angry at himself.

As Lewis deletes his email, he realizes that he is acting with the restraint of a warrior. He did not reflexively respond to his anger; he built a safe container (an unsent email) and then proceeded to examine the emotion.

Lewis composes a second email to the chief curator reminding him of their earlier discussions and agreement on a $1.7 million budget. Lewis says that in good conscience he cannot back a budget which, in his experience, will severely damage the museum's financial stability. Furthermore, he refuses to be responsible for putting his entire staff under the burden of an inevitable failure of reaching impossible goals. Lewis says that if the chief curator insists on the $1.9 million budget, he (Lewis) will have to go straight to the board and explain his position. If that fails, he will step down. Lastly, he points out that announcing a budget he has not approved to the board is a serious breach of protocol that will have to be addressed.

Before sending the email, Lewis checks with a close friend who agrees that this is his best course of action. When Lewis finally sends the email to the chief curator, he feels incredibly free and strong.

This is strong warrior practice with all three dimensions of the warrior at work: (1) Lewis has defined his personal ethic—that he is no longer willing to sit by and work under the burden of someone else's selfishly bad decision making; (2) Lewis shows his increased capacity to tolerate intense emotion—not only has he managed his anger by stopping himself from sending out his first (reflexive) email, but he has taken the time to examine his anger; and (3) Lewis has acted on his personal ethic and emotional truth by drawing a strong boundary with the chief curator.

Everything about an act like this can feel strange to a Transforming Person. It means walking toward conflict instead of hiding from it. It means holding painful emotions. It also means dealing from a place of power.

But this kind of action is also liberating. By taking a warrior stance, Lewis no longer has a need for resentment, bitterness, self-pity, or passive-aggressive behavior. Even though he is worried about the outcome of his disagreement, he finds that he feels strong and surprisingly light-hearted.

This is one of the curious paradoxes of Warrior Practice. Lewis has no idea how things will work out. The chief curator may see the wisdom of Lewis' stance or he may fight Lewis tooth and nail. But, after Lewis sends the email, it dawns on him that his position is quite powerful. Should the chief curator decide to fight him on the issues, Lewis feels confident that he is doing the right thing. If the board disagrees with him and Lewis decides to step down, he will not have to take part in the inevitable mess that the chief curator is creating. If the chief curator sees his wisdom, then Lewis has done an enormous service for the museum, drawn an excellent boundary with the chief curator, and gained a great deal of respect in the process.

WARRIOR SKILLS

Warrior skills are various methods of taking action that follow both heart and ethic. Some of these skills may already be in place or come quite naturally to the Transforming Person. Others may be exceptionally difficult and will require practice.

WARRIOR SKILLS
- Skillful aggression
- Setting strong and flexible boundaries
- Exercising restraint
- Strengthening the body
- Practicing emotionally open and assured sexuality
- Facing conflict with confidence
- Embracing power

Skillful Aggression

Aggression for the new warrior is an energy that he seeks to integrate and to master rather than to avoid: he is able to become angry or to remain calm, to hold his ground or go with the flow, doing so spontaneously and without stress.

—BOB AUBREY, *AIKIDO AND THE NEW WARRIOR*

Of all the warrior skills, the use of aggression is perhaps the most difficult for a Transforming Person to contemplate. The word "aggression" is often associated with forceful action and domination. Rather than looking at aggression as the active companion to hostility, we consider it a useful and often necessary characteristic of the warrior. For our purposes, aggression is a particular manner of pursuing a goal, characterized by great energy and determination.

The Transforming Person must accept that aggression is a part of their character. In fact, it's a necessary trait of all living creatures. Watch the purpose and persistence of a crow after a morsel, a puppy play-fighting with its siblings, or a three-year-old child trying to get attention. The Transforming Person must also come to terms with what is likely a lifetime of sublimating their aggression. Of course, suppressing aggression does not get rid of the desires that fueled it; it only resurfaces as passive-aggression.

We need look no further than the first two dimensions of the warrior for a guide to skillful aggression. First, skillful aggression must always be used in alignment with personal ethic. If we believe that what we are pursuing is right and good, aggression becomes a useful tool in the pursuit of our goals. Second, it is crucial to understand the emotions that underlie our desires. If we are not aware of the underlying emotions, our aggression will likely be unskillful and counterproductive. Take for example an argument in which we aggressively pursue changing the other person's mind. Underneath that pursuit, there is often a fear of the humiliation of being wrong. Fueled by fear, aggressive arguing becomes pointed and invasive, and will likely cause the other person to stop listening—precisely what we do *not* want to happen.

Remember how Lewis recognized his own anger in the earlier example? Having recognized his emotions, Lewis was able to use his aggression skillfully, pursuing an attainable budget without allowing his emotional state to undermine his goals.

Transforming People will very likely find that using skillful aggression is very satisfying because it is the act of letting loose our dreams. We are now free to acknowledge our desires, vigorously pursue them, and live with the consequences.

Setting Strong and Flexible Boundaries

Boundaries are the outward expression of our personal ethic with another person. If we do not believe gossip is healthy, then we make our preference clear to someone who tries to engage us in gossip. If we do not want our partner to look at our journal, we tell them that it is off limits.

Setting strong boundaries is hard for Nice People because it involves the risk of someone being unhappy with them. At first this will require a conscious decision and a lot of emotional effort, but it is always worth it.

Weak boundaries kill relationships and breed mistrust and contempt in other people. Strong boundaries inspire security and attraction in other people. When someone tells us that they do not want to be called before 9:00 a.m., we can feel secure in that knowledge and even admire the person for stating their preference. By contrast, consider how uncomfortable it is to ask someone if it's too early to call, hear the words, "it's fine," while their tone of voice makes it clear that it is *not* fine. The person is being "nice" to us, but it doesn't feel good, and we start to lose respect for them.

Notice that this section is about both strong *and* flexible boundaries. Boundaries are not useful if they are rigid and unchangeable. A good example is a child's bedtime. Children thrive with a consistent, regular bedtime (a good strong boundary). It makes them feel comfortable about their evening, knowing that their loving parents are in charge. However, a bedtime that cannot be occasionally changed becomes oppressive. There are special events in a child's life that should not be missed because of a bedtime, and the very lifting of the rule makes the event more exciting. In this way the child gets a double benefit from the boundary—both security and an occasional memorable occasion. If a boundary is strong and consistent, it will easily survive a minor breach.

Exercising Restraint

This is a skill that may at first appear quite natural for an introverted person, and quite difficult for an extrovert to master. However, both kinds of Nice People need to practice exercising restraint. An introvert may lack restraint when they accommodate another person's demands, while an extrovert's lack of restraint may include babbling to fill the quiet spaces or spilling their intimate secrets. In both cases, anxiety is the culprit.

A typical date provides all manner of opportunities to practice restraint. During the course of a single evening Lisa decides:

- Not to judge her date too harshly on his choice of tie (even though she is afraid what other people will think)
- Not to talk about her recent divorce (even though she feels an intense desire for sympathy)
- Not to accept her date's implicit invitation to agree with him that Arnold Schwarzenegger is a better actor than Tom Hanks (even though she really wants her date to like her)
- Not to invite her date over to her place (even though she is afraid of losing him)

In all of these scenarios we can see the need for a personal ethic. Lisa does not believe in lying to seek approval, so her date's Schwarzenegger/Hanks conversation is destined to fall flat. And, once again, the ability to tolerate emotion without reflexive action is crucial. Lisa is still hurting from her divorce and desperately wants sympathy. But she is able to tolerate and examine her pain. Rather than reflexively pour out her story to someone she does not yet trust, she keeps it to herself. Lisa's restraint reflects a strong Warrior Practice.

STRENGTHENING THE BODY

Years of being anxiously attached take a toll on a Nice Person's body. Anxiety plays a key role in major diseases, as well as chronic pain such as stomach upset, sleep disorders, obesity, and fatigue. And there are a host of lesser ailments—muscular pain, irregular bowel movements, rashes, teeth grinding, sexual dysfunction or disinterest, etc.—that Nice People simply live with and ignore as best they can. If they go to a doctor, they are likely to hear the words: "There's nothing wrong with you." But none of this is surprising if you consider a lifetime of constant worry, coupled with suppressed anger and grief. These emotions generate enormous energy, and when they are not acknowledged and dealt with, the energy lodges in the body.

The transformation of our hearts and minds is inseparable from the transformation of our bodies. As anxiety decreases, the possibilities for caring for the body and relieving pain increases. It is as if the Nice Person's body is a tightly wound and knotted ball of string. Each realization, each acceptance, each subtle transformation, untwists one snarl which in turns loosens the one next to it.

THE TRANSFORMING BODY

- Energy increases. Nice People squander energy by fretting about what other people are thinking and doing. Furthermore, low energy is often responsible for poor eating and lack of exercise.
- Emotional eating becomes more manageable. The urge to fill the empty place inside with food diminishes. Also, with more energy you may find you're more likely to take time with meals and eat healthy food.
- Use of mood-altering substances (caffeine, sugar, alcohol, other drugs) becomes more responsible. Like emotional eating, practicing self-care becomes easier as anxiety diminishes. Note: This is a different matter with an addiction, which requires a treatment model that specifically addresses the addictive process.
- Exercise increases. As you learn compassion and respect for yourself, exercise becomes a priority. With more energy, it's easier to do.

• Less pain. Lower anxiety, more exercise, better eating, and higher self-esteem often results in a reduction of pain.

Responsiveness to treatment/exercise/training increases. Less anxiety means less tension in your body. You will be less likely to be injured, and you will recover more quickly from injuries you do sustain. Your body will be more likely to change shape in response to training. Energy work (acupuncture, massage, reiki, etc.) will get better results because there will be fewer pockets of resistance.

A warrior strengthens the body through healthy emotional practice, and the emotional system through healthy physical practice

Each of these benefits affects the other and creates a snowball effect. Imagine this scenario: You are not in pain, and as a result, your Awareness Practice sharpens. As your awareness sharpens, you find that psychotherapy is more effective. Psychotherapy maximizes your Warrior Practice, which then benefits your exercise program. Exercising begins to clear your heart and head and helps you be a better parent…and on it goes.

Practicing Emotionally Open and Assured Sexuality

What Nice People have going for them as lovers is that they are emotionally empathic and often adept at pleasing a partner. What gets in their way is that they usually do not take responsibility for their own sexuality, and often do not know how to please themselves. Put simply, self-knowledge and confidence make for good sex, while self-doubt and anxiety do not.

In Chapter Nine we take a deeper look at why Nice People have so much trouble in relationships. In a nutshell, the Nice Person has unconscious expectations that a romantic partner will sooth their anxiety, supply ecstatic sex, and fill the empty places inside of them. At the same time, they are expecting to be treated badly, to carry the emotional burden for both people, and ultimately to be left. These conflicting sets of expectations translate into a secret one-sided agreement that Nice People make in their heads—"I'll give you everything and you won't leave me." This clandestine agreement inappropriately raises the importance, and therefore the anxiety, of sex.

Because the Nice Person is frightened to disappoint their lover, they give away the responsibility for their own sexual fulfillment. Waiting until the other person takes care of our needs is safer because it eliminates the possibility of rejection or failure.

- If you have a lover and are unhappy with the sex you are having, your goal will be to figure what you don't like about the sex (practicing nonjudgmental awareness), and then to address the issue with yourself and your lover.
- If you have no lover and want to have sex, your goal will be to find out why you don't have a lover (practicing nonjudgmental awareness) and figure how to go about finding one.
- If you find that you can't say no (this is a problem for both Nice Guys and Nice Girls), it is time for you to start paying attention to your own needs and setting better boundaries.

A barrier in all three of these scenarios is that Nice People often don't know what they want or like because they have always been focused on the other person. Sex, like every other part of life, can be experimented with, especially when the emotional consequences are no longer dire. The Transforming Person will learn what they enjoy by pleasuring themselves, talking and playing with their lover, and getting advice from their brotherhood or sisterhood.

In the first scenario (unhappy with the sex they are having) the Nice Person's fear is that they will try to talk to their lover about their sexual desires only to be scorned or shut down. Successful sexual communication requires that both lovers be conscious of creating a safe container. In this environment, the lovers learn to revel in their areas of mutual sexual interest while respecting their lover's differing sexual interests, even if they decide not to

It is the practice of a warrior to build a safe and loving environment for sex engage them. Ultimately we are looking for the bedroom to become a playroom where anxiety is checked at the door. Like every other endeavor in life, sex gets better with practice and, when the practice is play, it becomes fun. Here, performance is secondary. Each partner allows the other to fail, succeed, say "yes please," say "no thank you"—to experiment without judgment.

In the second scenario (wanting, but not getting sex) the Nice Person's fear is of finding themselves unlovable. Perhaps they are so terrified of being judged, losing love, feeling like a fool, being used, etc., that they do not want to risk looking for a lover. Or perhaps they have experienced rejection so often—because they are overweight, are extremely shy, have spent a lifetime being too nice, etc.—that they do not wish to be hurt again. The important words here are *nonjudgmental* and *compassionate*. To find a lover, the Nice Person will have to look unflinchingly, nonjudgmentally, and yet lovingly at their own state of being. They will also have to factor in the evolution of their transformation. While they are becoming more attractive, the *feeling* of being unattractive may linger. Lastly, they will need to explore their sexuality on their own.

The last scenario (learning to say no) can come as a great relief to the Transforming Person. This skill is an extension of the understanding that we are each responsible for our own sexuality. When a Transforming Person doesn't feel like having sex and says no, they are being loving to both themselves and their partner. It may not feel like it, but in this simple "no" are the messages: "I love me enough to take care of myself," "I respect you enough to be honest with you," and "I trust that our relationship does not rely on one sexual encounter." The lover of a Nice Person is often under an enormous strain because they aren't ever sure of when the Nice Person is being genuine or what the Nice Person wants. When the Transforming Person learns to say no, their lover can relax. "Ah, he respects me enough to trust me," or "Good, now I won't have to guess what she wants all the time."

The corollary to this is that as anxiety recedes, the Transforming Person no longer feels the urgency to perform, allowing both themselves and their lover to relax. Less urgency means that even if someone doesn't feel like having sex, or the sex of the moment isn't scintillating, it's really okay because that is simply how things are today. It means that cuddling without sex (without the anxiety that there won't be any more sex) becomes possible. It means that wild and experimental sex (without the anxiety that from now on all the sex will have to be wild and experimental) becomes possible.

An assured and open sexual environment helps the sex stay fresh and exciting

Facing Conflict with Confidence

We will dive fully into conflict in Chapter Twelve, Creative Conflict. For now we'll look at the warrior's attitude toward conflict. Conflict is inevitable and necessary. In fact it is a one of the tastiest ingredients in a relationship, and done correctly, it is a catalyst for intimacy.

For Nice People, however, it is anathema because it stimulates their core fears. "If I disagree, you will not love me." Warrior Practice in conflict involves boldly examining these underlying fears. This is easier said than done because Nice People have spent their lives finding clever ways for not only avoiding conflict but also hiding the avoidance techniques from themselves.

Any breach in our personal ethic can give rise to conflict. How well we contain the attending fear that arises will determine how free we are to observe our particular method of avoiding conflict. If we are tolerating our fear and aware of our avoidance techniques, then we are warriors who are ready to enter into conflict.

We can go back to the Lewis scenario and see that he was not ready to enter into a conflict until he looked at his emotions. He realized he was angry at the chief curator and rightly so. He realized that he was angry at himself for his years of being a Nice Guy. Once Lewis understood his emotions, he was able to clarify his motivation for the conflict. He knows that he is in the right because he has tested the problem against his personal ethic (and later with the advice of a friend). He also realizes that he is frightened of losing his job, but that the consequences of turning a blind eye are worse than being fired. Examining his fears has given Lewis the ability to confront the chief curator in a straightforward manner without making useless and damaging remarks.

Warrior Practice in conflict builds respect in friends, coworkers, family, and lovers. They know that they can trust you to be honest about what you want, confront them when you think they are out of line, and admit when you are acting badly or just plain wrong.

Embracing Power (Learning to Lead)

Embracing and wielding power is one of the main skills of Warrior Practice. This does not necessarily mean that all Transforming People will end up supervising crews, teaching classes, leading troops, or running boardrooms. Power may come in the brief moment that we speak up in a meeting and everyone gets quiet because they don't want to miss what we have to say. It may surface in the expectant look of an old friend waiting for advice. It may be the moment we turn to our spouse and calmly and powerfully say, "Let me take care of this."

Power is a natural outcome of Awareness and Desert Practice, which are the foundations for a calm, self-assured person. These traits are, for most people, as attractive as flowers are to bees. This very attractiveness can be alarming to a former Nice Person who has spent a lifetime radiating anxiety and harboring unconscious anger, which pushes people away.

Once the Transforming Person has begun to change their ingratiation habit and begun to accept that that they do indeed possess power, the three dimensions of the warrior apply. (1) Having a strong personal ethic is an absolute must for the skillful use of power. (2) Withstanding emotions without reflexive action is crucial to making strong and fair choices. And, of course, (3) a leader must act, and if their actions follow their personal ethic and heart, they will act well.

TRYING IT ON

As with most of these skills, leadership may be uncomfortable or frightening to Transforming People. In fact, it may be hard to imagine. It is helpful, therefore, to try on the behavior of a Transforming Person, even when our insides are screaming, "Liar!" Let's take the example of a baseball batter with a short, choppy swing. He was taught early on that if he chokes up on the bat he's got a better chance of making contact with the ball, but more often than not he gets thrown out trying to beat an infield grounder. So the batting coach has him move his hands down the bat and take a smoother, longer swing. The first time he goes up to the plate and tries this new technique, he feels uncomfortable. He doesn't feel like he has the same control and he's worried that he's going to flail away, strike out, and look like a fool. But he persists because he wants to improve. Pretty soon he starts to get some long singles and then some doubles. As the stance starts to feel familiar, he relaxes and he begins to hit with consistent power.

With Warrior Practice there will be mistakes, false starts, and setbacks. But eventually the skills become second nature, the practice of them pleasurable, and the warrior emerges.

Awareness, Desert, and Warrior Practice cannot be done alone. Remember in our earlier example when Lewis checks in with his friend before sending out the email to the chief curator? Each of us needs the support of friends in our transformation. Let's move on to Brotherhood and Sisterhood Practice.

yes yes

7

Brotherhood and Sisterhood Practice

The best mirror is an old friend.

—GEORGE HERBERT

All men need the brotherhood of other men. All women need the sisterhood of other women. While we also encourage friendship between men and women, same-gender friendship is an essential ingredient for Transforming People. The path of transformation has many twists and turns and it is easy to lose the way when we are alone. The Brotherhood and Sisterhood provide indispensable support and guidance.

> ## GAY, LESBIAN, BISEXUAL
> Homosexual and bisexual Transforming People need same-gender, *platonic* friends. The unique support of the Brotherhood or Sisterhood is undermined by the complex dynamics of sex and romance.

This practice will be enormously difficult for some and second nature to others depending on their personality (e.g., extrovert or introvert), their level of anxiety in relationships, and how they respond to societal pressures. We will discuss ways to overcome these difficulties later in the chapter, but first let's take a closer look at the benefits of Sisterhood and Brotherhood Practice.

WHY TRANSFORMING PEOPLE NEED SAME-GENDER FRIENDSHIP

Virtually all cultures share common ground when it comes to a perception of gender: women identify and group with other women, men with other men, and members of the opposite sex are, well, different. While friendships between women and men are important, getting together with same-gender friends, whether singly or in a group, can resonate deeply with our own sense of well-being.

Supports Masculinity and Femininity

Awareness, Desert, and Warrior Practices prompt a profound change in the way Transforming People view themselves. Among the many features of this emerging self-portrait is a new sense of masculinity or femininity. For our purposes, think of femininity or masculinity as a person's particular experience of his or her own gender. Men and women are different (biology, brain function, social experience) and our sisters and brothers understand these differences in an experiential way that the opposite sex cannot. We share an ancient secret with our gender-mates—a fundamental "you-get-what-it's-like" that helps us know that our masculinity or femininity is good and that we belong in the world.

Validates Unique Female or Male Communication Modes

Watch and listen to a group of men or a group of women hanging out together and you immediately recognize that they communicate differently.

Identifying the differences is tricky, and certainly there are exceptions to any generalization. However, research indicates that men and women use different parts of, and pathways in, their brains when communicating. Women are generally more verbal, better listeners, and more emotive and empathic. Men are generally more spatially and mechanically oriented, physically impulsive, and focused on abstract thinking. Women can often maintain several tasks and trains of thought. Men tend to focus on a single task or idea.

Communication is accomplished through the body: vocal chords, posture, gestures, expressions, etc. Men and women, then, must convey their ideas (which are already arrived at through a different process) with slightly but crucially different instruments. Nice People often get lost trying to accommodate the communication mode of the opposite sex. When a woman spends time with a female friend, it reminds her that she has her own particular way of communicating, which is important and valid. The same is true for men.

Provides a Masculine or Feminine Brand of Support, Clarity, and Accountability

We need friends who can listen to us. We need friends who can reflect our thoughts and emotions so that we can untangle them and achieve clarity. We need friends who are tough enough to call our bluff when we are acting badly. For a woman, the corroboration of three close women friends on an important issue is an unambiguously useful message. If these three friends share similar values, are loving, and are strong enough to speak their minds, then their advice counts. The fact that they are women provides important credibility because, as we have discussed, "they-know-what-it's-like." The same is true for men.

Provides Support and Reflection for Strong Desert Practice

Desert Practice will often evoke feelings of intense loneliness, triggering two defensive reflexes that are common to Nice People: (1) unhealthy isolation, and/or (2) escapist romantic or sexual fantasies and behaviors. While these paths may provide some temporary relief, they will not lead to a resolution of the troubled feelings, and will often make things worse. The Brotherhood and Sisterhood offer immunization against these reflexive pathways. The first shot-in-the-arm is obvious; if you're with your friends you are not in isolation.

The second immunization is more complex. One of the points of Desert Practice is to examine the kinds of escape the Nice Person turns to and the emotions that motivate them. This is tough to do alone because Nice People are adept at tricking themselves into ignoring and rationalizing their behavior. But it is difficult for a man to trick himself when his trusted brothers say: "She's stringing you along and you're ignoring it. You deserve better than that. It may hurt, but you've got to show yourself some respect and end this."

A good same-gender friendship helps the Transforming Person bear the pain of confronting his or her anxiety and escapist fantasies and behavior. If we have chosen our Sisters and Brothers well, then their advice and their ability to comfort us and listen to us is priceless.

Strengthens Romantic Relationships

Our culture, for many reasons, isolates us *with* our partners. There is a prevailing wisdom that our spouses and lovers are supposed to play every role in our lives: soul mate, lover, counselor, coparent, best friend, playmate, even business partner. This social one-stop-shopping is a fairy tale, and like most fairy tales it can turn problematic. Couples *without* Brotherhood and Sisterhood are under enormous strain for the following reasons:

- No matter how well matched a couple is, they will have some differing personality traits, interests, and desires that their partner either cannot or will not fulfill (i.e., she likes to rock climb, he collects model trains, she loves ballet, he prefers action films).
- Being constantly in someone else's presence, no matter how interesting they are, is a strain—conversation grows stale, the partner's habits grow irritating, the need for privacy builds up, etc.

- While in the presence of their partner, Transforming People will be recognizing and working with their recurring anxious-to-please tendencies. This is good work but it is also tiring work, and the frequent analysis of emotions, behavior, and memories can overtax the relationship.

The antidote for these isolated couple ailments is Brotherhood and Sisterhood Practice. A man who spends an afternoon with a couple of buddies and his teenage son at the baseball game has a good chance of coming home relaxed and happy. He got a break, and he got a dose of male energy. His partner, in turn, has taken the time to visit a women-only spa with a close friend. When they get back together, each will be generally refreshed and grounded. They may also find upon returning that they have new ideas or stories to share.

A close friend can be particularly supportive of a romantic relationship. Each of us needs a safety-valve and confidante. When we get deep inside our "nice" behavior in a relationship, we need to have a sister or brother we can go to and say: "Is he/she just being a jerk? Or is it me? Am I doing my Nice Person thing here?" If we have chosen our Sister or Brother because we trust their judgment, and if their judgment is time-tested and based on respect for us, then their advice is hard to ignore.

Getting Our Needs Met

Nice People live in a state of love-deprivation—a perpetual purgatory of longing in which the fulfillment of their needs feels just out of reach. When we have strong same-gender friends, we start to become aware that they are meeting some of our needs. It can be a strange realization for the Transforming Person that working on the remodel with their friend was precisely the thing that they needed. At first, they may feel both fulfilled *and* unfulfilled (a hangover from their life-long state of longing). As the Transforming Person learns to accept having their needs satisfied by their sisters and brothers, they can bring the experience back to enrich their romantic relationships.

OBSTACLES TO BROTHERHOOD AND SISTERHOOD PRACTICE

Brotherhood and Sisterhood Practice can have some obstacles including:

- Expectations of same-gender friends as competitors
- Early experiences of being hurt or betrayed by same-gender friends
- Feelings of inadequacy in the presence of same-gender contemporaries
- Nice People in long-term relationships tend to focus exclusively on their partners, dropping old friends by the wayside and not attempting to make new friends
- Partners jealous of time and connection with other friends

Most of us, in our childhoods, have experienced any or all of the first three obstacles. They are not the fondest memories—school-age rivalries, competitions, and exclusions—which, because we were Nice-People-in-training, inevitably ended in our giving up, taking care of everyone, bowing out, and getting hurt. The desperate need for friendship made us vulnerable to these kinds of injuries.

As we transform and our desperation fades, we find that we can start to choose our friends more carefully. Simultaneously, our awareness grows much more acute, and we become capable of sensing our own feelings of competitiveness or inadequacy, as well as weeding out untrustworthy friends.

Transforming People in romantic relationships need to talk with their partners about Brotherhood/Sisterhood Practice. After all, it is not unreasonable that a spouse might be concerned that Brotherhood/Sisterhood Practice might crowd out couple time or family birthdays or church. When a couple is supporting and encouraging one another, it makes the Practice not only more effective, but also a lot of fun.

Partners should be encouraged to express their feelings about Brotherhood/Sisterhood Practice, to talk about their excitement or fear, and to have input on how the Practice will be carried out

If, on the other hand, a partner tries to make a Transforming Person feel guilty for getting together with same-gender friends or tries to make it so difficult that it isn't worth the effort, this behavior must be addressed.

Obstacles Particular to Brotherhood

There is much about our experience as men that can only be shared with, and understood by, other men. There are stories we can tell only to those who have wrestled in the dark with the same demons and been wounded by the same angels. Only men understand the secret fears that go with the territory of masculinity.

—SAM KEEN, *FIRE IN THE BELLY*

Our society particularly discourages men from getting together with other men. Among the difficulties are:
- Aversion to talking about feelings with other men
- Homophobia
- The perception that there are limited options for men getting together

For many men, the very phrase "talking about feelings" sounds uncomfortable—it smacks of something that women do, and it doesn't feel right. The solution is to reframe the picture and talk about experiences. A Transforming Man needs to find a Brotherhood that includes a few men he can deeply trust, friends that he can talk to from time-to-time about what he is experiencing. It's helpful if he can express his emotions in the style that fits him. Some men may be quite comfortable with saying, "I'm angry," "I'm pissed off," "I'm frustrated," "I'm excited." Others may feel more comfortable with metaphors: "I felt like she kicked me in the nuts," "My stomach dropped out of me," "I'm ready to explode." For some, it will be sufficient to relate the experiences and let the emotions speak for themselves.

Homophobia, as an obstacle to the Brotherhood, is specifically about the fear of being perceived as gay and being attacked or snubbed because of it. This fear can cause all manner of uncomfortable feelings when men are trying to befriend other men. It affects straight men and gay men; it affects men who are uncomfortable with homosexuality and men who are completely at ease with homosexuality. What is required is to accept that a cultural discomfort exists and may make Brotherhood Practice difficult. The challenge is to go ahead and do it anyway.

There is a perception that men have limited options for getting together. This is mostly because socializing is thought of as a feminine activity. As we will see in the section below, men and women tend to have a different orientation towards friendship. Men often prefer to have an activity, task, or hobby to focus on when hanging out with their buddies. Thinking about it this way opens up a world of possibilities—racquet ball, a Sunday football game, a chess match, a three-mile run, a charity fundraiser, fishing, and the list goes on.

DIFFERENCES IN WOMEN'S AND MEN'S FRIENDSHIP VALUES

Women and men tend to attach different values to friendship. For women, a relationship is often an end in itself—they get together to enjoy the company of another woman. Men tend to organize a relationship around work, sports, or play. This is by no means universal, but it is useful to note and important to understand that both orientations are valid.

THE VARIETIES OF BROTHERHOOD AND SISTERHOOD PRACTICE

There is no formula for determining what kinds of friendships comprise an ideal Brotherhood or Sisterhood. It is a fluid practice, changing as friends and affiliations become more or less important and available. What we can do is discuss the possibilities.

VARIETIES OF BROTHERHOOD AND SISTERHOOD PRACTICE

This chart is a buffet—pick and choose what fits your personality and lifestyle.

Mutual interest groups:	Groups brought together by a shared activity or interest: sports, politics, religion, hobbies, parenting, etc.
Events or retreats:	Time-specific gathering for a particular purpose: health, spiritual, professional, travel, therapeutic, artistic, etc.
Mentors, teachers, students:	Teaching or receiving guidance and instruction.
Family members:	A good familial relationship can offer friendship and/or guidance along with the unique understanding of a shared heritage.
Friendship groups:	Smaller groups of friends.
Close friendships:	Individuals with whom you feel a close bond and a higher level of trust.

All Brotherhood and Sisterhood is valuable (yes, it's important to go shopping with the girls or bowling with the guys or vice versa). However, we believe that having a few close friends is crucial to the other six practices presented in this book.

EVALUATING BROTHERHOOD/SISTERHOOD NEEDS

The Transforming Person must first evaluate their Brotherhood/Sisterhood needs by asking the following questions:

What relationships would help most with my transformation?
Who do I have in my life that currently meets those needs?

Connor is extroverted and making friends comes naturally to him. However, he recently got married and moved to a different state. He has been missing his college buddies and in particular, his best friend. He has joined a men's soccer league, but he would like to find a smaller group of guys to hang out with to share some laughs and let off steam. He also wants to find one or two guys that he can talk to about things that are on his mind (like how his job is not going as well as he'd like and how frightened his wife has been about the move).

Joyce is an introvert and finds it very difficult to meet people. She is divorced and has a very good relationship with her two teenage daughters. She works at night, which allows her to pursue her passion for gardening in her backyard during the day. While Desert Practice has been a piece of cake for Joyce, she has found Awareness Practice and particularly Warrior Practice to be challenging. She is frightened about Sisterhood Practice, but feels ready to give it a try. Her current circle includes her two daughters and her sister with whom she is very close. The thought of being with a group of women feels overwhelming to Joyce, but she would like to find another close friend outside her family.

FINDING BROTHERS AND SISTERS

Both Connor and Joyce have evaluated their needs and are ready to take a step in the Brotherhood/Sisterhood Practice. But the next step may be difficult. Connor's wife is already feeling jealous of his time with the soccer league, so he's uneasy about how he's going to find time to hang out with a friend. There are a couple of guys on his soccer team that he thinks might be good candidates, but the competitive, masculine atmosphere makes it hard to figure out a way to bring up something beyond Manchester United and where to get a good cheeseburger. Connor does not consider himself homophobic, but at the same time, he senses that there is a careful external show of heterosexuality on the soccer team, which makes him uneasy about bringing up the idea of getting to know some of the guys better.

While Connor's obstacles are external, Joyce's are more of the internal variety. Joyce has been aware of her introverted nature for some time, and while it is a blessing in many ways, it makes it hard to cultivate relationships. She wishes fervently that friends could be selected like gardening tools on an Internet shopping site—a couple of clicks and three days later your new friend arrives in the mail. Going out and meeting people seems fraught with unhappy possibilities like saying something stupid, being rejected, or befriending someone awful who she can't get rid of.

Little Steps

Joyce and Connor need to ask themselves the question: "What is the smallest change I can make that still feels like it would make a difference?" This bite-size model is handy for any practice because it helps get around the this-is-too-big-and-I-don't-know-where-to-start problem. Friendship doesn't happen overnight, but it won't happen at all if we don't make a start. Little steps will get the job done.

Joyce has written down her ideas in a journal:

- Join a gardening group
- Join a book club (she's an avid reader)
- Join her sister's monthly women-only hiking group
- Do more work at her girls' school (figuring to meet some other moms there)

What is the smallest change I can make that still feels like it would make a difference?

All four of these ideas feel too big to Joyce so she invents smaller steps to get started.

- Research gardening groups on the Internet
- Research book clubs on the Internet
- Talk to her sister about the hiking group
- Look at the school activities for the year

Joyce looks over the list and picks the two options she is most comfortable with: researching gardening groups on the Internet and talking to her sister. These are steps that she feels are at once manageable and in the right direction.

Connor makes some notes on a yellow sticky note at work and pops them in his wallet:

- Talk to his wife about what he wants
- Invite the whole soccer team over for a barbecue (figuring that in a more relaxed atmosphere he'll get to know some of the guys better)
- Call his university and find out if there is an active alumni association in the area
- Investigate a karate dojo that is a few blocks from his house (Connor has always wanted to try karate and he's thinking it might be a good place to meet other health-conscious friends.)

That evening Connor talks to his wife. Because they are working together at having a conscious relationship, they are able to have a good discussion about how anxious they both feel living in a new city without family and friends. Connor's wife agrees that he should be looking for close male friends and that she needs to find some women friends. Together, they make a list of ideas for her to get more connected; meanwhile, Connor revises his own list:

- Call his university and find out if there is an active alumni association in the area
- Investigate a karate dojo and possibly join when soccer season ends
- Wait until the boxes are unpacked and then invite the whole soccer team, including their partners, over for a barbecue so that both he and his wife will have an opportunity to meet potential friends

Of course there are myriad ways to do Brotherhood and Sisterhood Practice. Some Transforming People have no same-gender friends at all and will be starting from scratch. Some Transforming People may already have numerous same-gender friends, and their goal may be to simply strengthen one or two of these ongoing relationships. Others may have same-gender friendships left over from their "Nice Person days" which are harmful to them, and may be faced with the difficult task of letting go of those relationships.

QUALITIES TO LOOK FOR IN BROTHERS AND SISTERS

True friendship is a plant of slow growth, and must undergo and withstand the shocks of adversity before it is entitled to the appellation.

—GEORGE WASHINGTON

One of the goals of Brotherhood/Sisterhood Practice is to find a few close friends, and more specifically, finding at least one person with whom to speak the truth. Friendship is indeed a "plant of slow growth" and we cannot tell when we meet someone whether they will become a close friend. But since Transforming People usually have a history of unbalanced relationships, it is useful to give thought to what we are looking for in a sister or brother. Consider that men and women may be seeking somewhat different qualities. Men often find that they cherish courage and integrity above other qualities in their brothers, while women may prize such qualities as emotional openness and honesty. This is a generalization, but it is useful for stimulating thought.

QUALITIES TO LOOK FOR IN BROTHERS AND SISTERS

- They are working on themselves (transforming)
- You share a mutual respect with them
- They have the ability to listen and appreciate being listened to
- You share some values and interests with them
- They have the courage to speak their mind

PRACTICING FRIENDSHIP

I do not wish to treat friendships daintily, but with the roughest courage. When they are real, they are not glass threads or frostwork, but the solidest thing we know.

—RALPH WALDO EMERSON

Strangely, for all the pitfalls that anxious attachment sets in the way of friendship, it also plays a role in developing the best qualities of a good friend. Friendship requires empathy, kindness, patience, humor, and loyalty—qualities that Nice People often have in abundance. These characteristics will become more prominent as the Transforming Person develops the aspects of their personality that have been retarded, such as individuation, strength, confidence, calmness, and self-esteem.

Bring a Warrior Sensibility

Nice People have a habit of being submissive in relationships in order to ensure that they will be liked or at least not left. This "niceness" ultimately undermines Brotherhood and Sisterhood relationships, which rely on a mutual strength. Here's an example of a conversation between two writers in the early stages of planning a book called *Anxious to Please*—we'll call them Wilberforce and Friedkin to protect their identities.

Wilber: Tell you what, since you know more about this subject, let's assume that I'll do the bulk of the typing and research and you'll contribute the ideas.

Fried: Whoa. Wait a minute. That doesn't feel right. I've got to tell you, that sounds pretty much like a Nice Guy deal. Do you remember in seventh grade when we worked on that play and you wrote the whole thing, but we both got credit for it? It sounds like that.

Wilber: You're right. I just went completely Nice Guy on you. That's how I do it—I'll be the silent martyr/saint and support us both, and then you'll be my friend. Even worse, it relieves me of my responsibility to contribute the full force of my opinions. It's my marriage all over again.

Fried: Hey, buddy, I'm not asking for a diamond ring or anything here. Seriously though, it makes me feel pretty weird when you do that, like you think I can't carry my weight. Basically, I want to be treated like an adult—equal-to-equal.

Wilber: Yup, you're right. You got it. Fifty-fifty.

It is important to note that it was not as easy as this shortened version makes it sound for Friedkin to realize what he was doing. Fortunately, he had been working for some time on Awareness Practice so he recognized the behavior when it was pointed out to him.

It is Warrior Practice that allows Transforming People to hold up their side of a friendship, to support a friend in pain or stand their ground when a friend is being demanding.

Lead without Domination, Follow without Submission

This concept can apply to individual friendships, groups of friends, or larger gatherings. In any endeavor, leading and following are honorable and necessary roles to play, but each has an associated trap for the Transforming Person. Anxiety plants a niggling worry in the Nice Person's head that if she or he is not in complete control, everything will fall apart. The trick is to keep a watch for the anxiety, let it rise and fall, but not act on it. Good leaders are capable of both listening to and incorporating the skills and ideas of others, and making calm, timely, and firm decisions based on their own judgment.

To Nice People, following feels similar to submitting and they can easily fall into lifetime patterns of over-functioning, silent service, and suppressed anger. But a good follower is capable of carrying out instructions effectively without losing her or his sense of individuality.

Communicate with Respect and with the Expectation of Respect in Return

When we are anxious, we are constantly concerned about ourselves and how to soothe our anxiety. This makes it very difficult to truly focus on another person, appreciate their differences and similarities, enjoy their fine points

Practice listening to the best part of other women or men

and have compassion for their faults. As anxiety diminishes, patience increases, as does empathy and listening skills. When we listen to the best part of another woman or man, we learn to respect them.

We must expect the same respect from our friends; otherwise, the friendship is not balanced. We need Sisters and Brothers who are willing to set their own issues aside and listen to us, encourage us, grant us grace, and treat us with respect.

Identify Your Own Emotional Style, While Accepting a Wide Range of Emotional Styles in Your Friends

While Nice People are worrying about what other people are thinking or feeling, they are unable to observe the differences between their own process and that of someone else. A not-uncommon Nice Person scenario goes like this:

Ms. Nice: "It is so weird to think that I've been anxious all of my life and didn't know it. All the pieces fit together like a puzzle—the back problems, the perfectionist stuff, the nerves, the feeling left out, the feeling completely responsible for every relationship...of course that's how everybody feels, I guess."

Therapist: (Shakes her head.) "No. That's not how everybody feels. A lot of people aren't filled with anxiety."

Ms. Nice: (Laughs, a bit nervously.) "That's awful. I mean it's great that not everybody is anxious, but...why me? And why did I think everyone was just the same as me?"

As we grow more comfortable with our uniqueness, we are able to notice and enjoy a wide variety of thought processes and emotional styles in those around us. Perhaps we experience emotion immediately and it makes us laugh or cry or pump our fists or want to hug someone; then that's our style and it's marvelous. Perhaps we have a close friend who experiences emotions slowly and internally. At first we may think that they are holding back, that they are "in a mood," or even that they are angry with us. But as we calm down, we can begin to appreciate their emotional style and even learn to partake of it, enjoying a different way of savoring life.

Humor, Grace, and Patience

It is one of the blessings of old friends that you can afford to be stupid with them.

—RALPH WALDO EMERSON

One of the very best things about Sisterhood and Brotherhood Practice is sharing laughter. There is no more joyful sound then the pealing laughter, the uncontrollable giggles, or the wicked cackling of women who care about each other. There is nothing more satisfying then the grins, the guffaws, the chortles, the sheer physicality of men sharing a joke. Laughter loosens us, oils us, and makes us run better. When our eyes are still wet with tears of laughter, we are able to see our Brothers and Sisters clearly and appreciate them fully.

This is not only about telling jokes, but about developing a sense of grace. We have talked about grace in conjunction with nonjudgmental awareness, but it is also a crucial element in friendship. Grace is about tolerance (which includes humor and patience) with our own and our friends' mistakes. Extending grace to a friend who has acted badly or foolishly is a hallmark of strong Brotherhood and Sisterhood Practice.

When we can have a sense of humor about our weaknesses, our stubbornness, and our anxiety, then change and healing are imminent

Appropriate patience can be a challenge for Transforming People. As Nice People, we were used to enduring bad behavior and not speaking up when something bothered us. Now, when we recognize that something is bothering us, we are likely to do something about it. The difficulty lies in knowing when to act. If a Brother is repeating a behavior that we can see is leading to harm, then we have to talk to him about it. But if he makes a single off-the-cuff remark, perhaps we can have some patience and let it slide. Knowing when to have patience requires an awareness of our own emotions. We may find it particularly difficult to bear our brothers and sisters who are indulging in Nice Person behavior because it sends a direct line of voltage into our own anxiety. However, our Sisters and Brothers need time to change just as we do, and patience is sometimes the greatest gift we can give them.

Our Brothers and Sisters are indispensable in every phase of transformation, not the least of which is the next chapter, Family Practice, which brings us around again to our beginnings. This time we will be giving our family of origin a story and a context.

8

Family Practice

Those who know ghosts tell us that they long to be released from their ghost life and led to rest as ancestors. As ancestors they live forth in the present generation, while as ghosts they are compelled to haunt the present generation with their shadow life...

—PSYCHOANALYST HANS LOEWALD

FROM GHOSTS TO ANCESTORS

The central theme of anxious attachment is *relationship*. The chronic anxiety of the Nice Person originates with problems in the first relationship of life—between child and parents—and is perpetuated by relational patterns within the family of origin (i.e., the family in which a person grew up). While other significant relationships continue to shape the anxiously attached person in both positive and negative ways, the baseline is the family. The buried memories and patterns of this familial past become ghosts that haunt the psyche, intruding into current life with unwelcome fits of emotions and habits of thought.

Transformation, too, is fostered by relationships. The process of healing and growth requires the infusion of love and compassion from a multitude of sources, particularly partners and friends. Therapeutic and spiritually-oriented relationships can play crucial roles as well.

Family Practice focuses on the relationships within the Transforming Person's family of origin. By examining the family's past as a way of understanding the present, the Transforming Person can make changes that give the future a new direction. The haunting ghosts are laid to rest and become simply remembered ancestors.

Family Practice consists of two branches. The first involves a look at the history of the family, leading to the creation of a storyline: "This is how I came to be who I am today." This story is fluid, evolving over time as new insights and information become understood. The story becomes an invaluable resource for the Transforming Person.

The second branch of Family Practice is about assessing and changing one's way of being with family members. Most Nice People don't feel fully accepted by their families, and have spent a lifetime adapting in the vain attempt to find a sense of belonging. This part of Family Practice helps the Transforming Person learn to stop adapting and to become an authentic presence in the family.

LAUNCHING

The developmental stage of leaving home and becoming an autonomous adult is common to virtually all cultures. *Launching*, as it is known, establishes the person as a separate being who carries both the right and the responsibility to determine their own destiny. As an adult discovers who they are apart from their family, they establish a secure base within themselves. From this base they can build healthy relationships with friends, partners, and family that sustain them in a respectfully interdependent way, different from the child-parent dependency of early life.

Launching, then, is an essential element of developing an internal sense of security, making it a matter of paramount importance for people who are recovering from anxious attachment.

Most adult Nice People are stuck in a "half-launched" state—they are usually on their own in most concrete ways (have a job, separate home, etc.), but their emotional connections with family have not transitioned to a truly adult form. Unsatisfied by their childhood and still yearning for security, they find it difficult to accept that they are now fully responsible for addressing their own needs.

The great challenge of launching is supposed to be about the tug between the comfort of home and the irresistible call of the wild blue yonder—two good things beckoning from opposite directions. But insecure rocketeers (aka Nice People) are ambivalent about both the past and the future, lacking confidence that they can find what they need in either place. For them, the achievement of launching will require that they come to accept the limits and losses of their childhood, while also assuming responsibility for their own life.

The Differentiated Self

The goal of launching is to become fully oneself, neither adapting to nor rebelling against the family of origin.

The field of psychology has borrowed a term from cellular biology—"differentiation"—to refer to the way in which people blossom into becoming who they truly are. Like cells, we differentiate by manifesting our own unique nature. In particular, we do this by becoming able to think, feel, and act in ways that are separate from those around us.

Unlike cells, our process of differentiation happens slowly, often by taking a step backward for every two or three steps forward. We work out our growth in relationships with the people that hold the greatest emotional sway with us—our parents, siblings, and spouses or lovers.

The need for differentiation shows up in two forms of relationship that we could call "Sun and Moon" and "Teeter-Totter."

Sun and Moon. In this relationship, one person is "in orbit" around the other person (or people). The Moon avoids conflict with the Sun by adapting, acquiescing, and appeasing (sound like a Nice Person?). The Sun may appear to be more differentiated, but in fact they are as dependent on the orbiting Moon as the Moon is on them.

Teeter-Totter. Here the two people are fused in a defiant opposition, like the two ends of a teeter-totter. When one goes up, the other is compelled to go down. When one says "We must do such-and-such!" the other responds with "No, let's do something else!"

In each of the forms above, a person cannot discover what they really think and feel because they are constantly adapting (Sun and Moon) or opposing (Teeter-Totter). True intimacy between family members, partners, or friends can only happen when the people involved are differentiated.

LETTING GO OF THE PAST

Family Practice includes letting go of the past—giving up claim to receiving what was wanted in childhood. To do this we must accomplish two things:

1. Acknowledge our losses—admitting to ourselves what we needed but didn't receive from our family during childhood
2. Accept that our time for fulfilling these needs from our family is now past, and that we must take the mantle of responsibility for our own life

These two steps are major developmental accomplishments, and the degree of difficulty and complexity involved can vary widely from one person to another.

STUDYING THE FAMILY OF ORIGIN

At the foundation of Family Practice is the careful study of one's family of origin. We endeavor to see our families with new eyes, observing both past and present dynamics from a nonjudgmental perspective. As with all efforts of awareness, the study of the family is foremost a matter of studying ourselves, noticing our own patterns of mind, heart, body, and behavior as we interact with our own kin.

The best posture for studying the family is one of openness and compassion. This is not always so easily done. Each remembered event and every new perspective can trigger emotions that make us want to pull back or lash out. Our pain and longing compel us to categorize family members (including ourselves) as scoundrels, heroes, or victims. To see the family with new eyes requires ample amounts of patience and courage.

The techniques described here are drawn from the rich tradition of family therapy, and represent time-tested approaches to examining the family of origin. Each technique looks at the family from a different angle and elicits different kinds of information, so it can be valuable to use more than one.

HOW TO STUDY YOUR FAMILY OF ORIGIN

- **Collect stories and perspectives from as many family members as possible.** Most people are willing and even eager to tell stories about the family. Sometimes these are from personal experience; sometimes they are lore that has been handed down from previous generations. Whether the conversations are informal or structured, people will often be enthusiastic enough about a project to gather family stories and will gladly contribute.

  Everyone has a unique way of seeing, remembering, and passing on stories. Each story says something about the person telling it, so pay attention to what the storyteller chooses to emphasize or leave out. The swapping of stories can open new lines of communication and help family members to see one another in different ways.

- **Identify important family roles.** Some roles in the family are obvious, such as breadwinner or homemaker. Some are more subtle. Map out who played what roles in your family, keeping in mind that everyone plays more than one role and that these roles can change over time. Remember to include yourself and whatever roles you think you might have played. It's okay that your perspective is subjective; this is an exploration of your own way of seeing yourself and your family. Consider how the family might change if you were to step into a different role.

- **Identify important family alliances.** In every family (particularly in the extended family that includes aunts, uncles, grandparents, etc.) there are alliances. Parents aren't always on the same side, and even twin siblings can align with different factions. These alliances play a significant factor in how family dynamics unfold.

Examine each relationship within your family, mapping out the different ways that people align with each other. Particular issues can draw sharper battle lines. Even so, in most families the blocs remain subtle, and the alignments can shift.

- **Examine the normal stages of separation/individuation during childhood, and how these were handled and interpreted by parents.** Over the span of childhood there are at least three key stages when the child is developing their sense of separateness and independence. The first is from about eighteen months to three years of age; the second occurs around puberty (usually around eleven to fourteen years old); and the third happens when the child is launching (about eighteen to twenty-two years old). Each of these stages has unique developmental tasks, but the overall purpose is still the same: the child must find the level of separateness and autonomy that they need while still being able to feel connected to and loved by the family.

  Problems arise in these stages when the children don't feel safe enough to take self-directed actions. If the parents react too harshly (shaming or terrifying a child, for example), or with too much indifference (neglecting or abandoning a child), their children's development toward launching may be stunted. To study this dynamic within your family of origin, consider what these stages were like for you and your siblings; think about the levels of conflict and affection that were exchanged between parents and children; reflect on the parental values that came into play.

- **Outline patterns and themes that pass from generation to generation.** Information gathered about preceding generations of your family can reveal interesting similarities and differences that trace through the family like a stream. You may find a high frequency of mental illness, cancer, or substance abuse; a pattern of strong women and weak men, or ambitious entrepreneurs; themes of spiritual devotion or hard work ethic or victimhood; and so on. Some things skip generations, as one family reacts to reverse the trend of the previous one, which is subsequently reversed by the next, and so on.

These patterns and themes hold meaning for the extended family. In fact, there are often family myths about them: "We Hamsterfields have always been good with money," or "Ever since Great-Great-Grandpa Bestertester sold the farm, no one in this family has had any decent luck." Mostly, the meanings are subtler and tend to be invisible to family members—someone might grow up knowing that "In this family, everyone goes to college," but they may not connect it to attitudes formed three generations earlier by immigrant parents who felt humiliated about their inability to speak English.

CREATING A COHESIVE FAMILY STORY

Every good story has a theme. The organizing idea brings relevance to the events and offers insight as the natural fruit of the story. Check out five biographies of Abraham Lincoln and you will find five different ways of narrating his life, each with different emphases to illustrate the theme of the biographer, yet each drawing from the same basic facts of Lincoln's life.

We make meaning from our own history and that of our family, whether we are aware of it or not. The process of creating a narrative about the family history helps us by organizing the mélange of memories, myths, and feelings into a form that is accessible. As new information and insights occur, old understandings can be replaced, allowing for breakthroughs that might not otherwise be possible.

KEYS FOR CREATING AND UPDATING YOUR FAMILY STORY

- Draw from your family history with a willingness to consider multiple ways of interpreting events
- Consider cultural dynamics, current and past, that have influenced the course of your family history
- Allow for ongoing events to modify your understanding of yourself and your family
- Assemble a storyline of personal heritage—building an evolving theory of how the family history contributed to your own development.

CHANGING YOURSELF MEANS CHANGING HOW YOU ARE IN YOUR FAMILY

A belief that often lingers unnoticed is the idea that we can change without affecting our primary relationships. We hope to insulate our loved ones from the major shifts that we are navigating in our own lives. But relationships are the place that we most poignantly experience the effects from the change within, and nowhere is that more true than with our families. Our transformation is going to affect our families.

Most Nice People feel shaky about being accepted by their families. Usually this is not a question of whether they will be invited for Thanksgiving; it's about whether they will be received as they are without having to put on a different persona. Nice People have been adapting and accommodating for a long time, and they first learned to do this when growing up in their families.

The need for acceptance and approval from the family (especially parents) is extremely durable, and (try as we might) we can't just resolve it by deciding that "it shouldn't be that important to me." Many people choose the option of relocating to a far-off place, but this only freezes the state of alienation.

BENEFITS AND LIABILITIES OF BEING CLOSE TO YOUR FAMILY

The business community often uses the term "Cost/Benefit Analysis" to describe the process of weighing the positives of something against the negatives. An essential component of Family Practice is this kind of assessment of one's place in the family of origin with the goal of deciding how healthy or unhealthy it is to be close to them.

It's important to understand that this is not a moral assessment (as in, "Are they good or bad?"), but an evaluation of the degree of health. This assessment is done on an ongoing basis: families evolve, and an environment that is toxic today may become beneficial in the future.

Potential benefits of being close to one's family of origin include:
- A greater sense of connection with family
- Increased feeling of safety

- Greater access to family resources
- Awareness and appreciation for one's heritage
- Reduced likelihood of isolation

Potential liabilities include:
- Involvement in toxic relationships
- Diminished feelings of self-worth
- Overexposure of yourself and your children to abusive elements (verbal, physical, sexual, or substance)
- Too much family interference with your life decisions
- Loss of a distinct sense of self

THE END OF ADAPTING

Gandhi said, "You must be the change you want to see in the world." It follows that a person can only promote change in their family by behaving in new ways. For the Transforming Person, this means changing the central "nice" habit of relating to the family: adapting in order to belong.

The important phrase here is "*...in order to belong.*" Adapting, like all nice behaviors, can be healthy when it's used at the right time and (especially) for the right reason. Possibly the worst application of adapting is in the effort to gain acceptance. Beyond the damage to self-esteem, it is an exercise in futility: if you censor yourself in order to be accepted, it isn't really *you* who is being accepted.

How can we get our family to love us for who we really are? The sad news is we can't. Paradoxically, accepting that difficult truth is a key to healing: "If I cannot make them love me, then I also cannot *lose* their love by being myself. By being true to myself and by acting in accordance with my own perceptions and integrity, I am presenting the only 'me' that I have. The members of the family will either accept me or they won't." As we give up the pattern of adapting in order to be accepted by the family, a strange thing happens: we find ourselves seeing the family members for who they are—for all of their shortcomings, weaknesses, and frailties, as well as their strengths and good qualities that we might have underestimated. We begin to accept that this is where we came from.

By coming to accept ourselves *and* our family, we can form a more loving approach to our connection with the family. As we come to understand what our family is capable of giving us, we can decide how much or little to invest in those relationships. The feeling of belonging that we sought from our family is becoming relocated to a more secure place—within ourselves.

WAYS TO CHANGE RELATIONSHIPS WITHIN THE FAMILY OF ORIGIN

- Develop resource network outside of family to support your change of stance within the family.
- When possible, initiate conversations that explore new insights, especially about family history and patterns of dysfunction.
- Give particular focus to family members who are also interested in change.
- Practice grace and compassion toward yourself and your family members.
- Allow time for change to take place.

Nicole, age thirty-four, has struggled with insecurity and anxiety her entire life. Despite professional accomplishments and personal growth, she has always felt that she is a disappointment to her parents and her older brother, Grant. Her father and brother are high-achievers, and no one in the family is particularly generous with praise.

Recently, Nicole and Grant were both staying with their parents during the holidays as has been their habit. This time, however, Nicole decided to practice being more candid. When her mother asked about her life, Nicole felt the impulse to say that everything was fine; instead, she talked about her fears for the future, her ambivalence about being single, her frustration with her career. Later, when Grant suggested they order Chinese, she took a deep breath and admitted that, though she'd never told them, she actually didn't particularly care for Asian cuisine. When her father went off on a rant about regional politics, she took issue with a few of his points and expressed her own perspective.

The results were mixed. Her mother seemed uneasy at first with her daughter's candor; but by the end of the holiday she had relaxed, and found herself telling stories from her own life that Nicole had never before heard. Everyone laughed heartily at her food confession, and she found herself enjoying (rather than hating) the good-natured ribbing that followed. Her father, on the other hand, seemed to be quite uncomfortable with the new assertiveness that she showed in confronting his politics, and threw a few demeaning comments at her before walking out of the room. Nicole felt terrible, but also began to understand more about why she'd always been a Nice Girl, afraid to express her own opinions.

Over time, she has realized that her father's behavior isn't really about her at all, but is more about his own defensiveness. Nicole is growing, and the effects that radiate out to her family are creating a feedback loop that brings about more growth for everyone. As she learns to give up the pattern of adapting, she is coming to see and accept her family for who they are.

THE FRUIT OF THE FAMILY TREE

Relationship is at the core of being human—as the conduit for learning and growth; as the fire that warms us, the milk that feeds us, and the serum that heals us. The families we inherit as children place an inevitable stamp on us, for better and for worse. The task of making sense of that heritage, and particularly of making *use* of it, is an ongoing endeavor that can change our lives.

The ways that we are formed by our families of origin continually affect (and *in*fect) our other relationships. Nowhere is this influence felt more powerfully than in the realm of romance. Anxious attachment invariably leads to a host of fantasies and projections that permeate romantic attachments for Nice People, leading to confusion, pain, and damage. Disillusionment Practice reveals the tools for disentangling the emotions and behaviors that can make romance such a calamity for Nice People.

yes yes

9

Disillusionment Practice

The first serious impediments to the growth of authentic love between the sexes is the sentimental, romantic way we think about love.

—SAM KEEN, *A FIRE IN THE BELLY*

We've already looked at how Nice People's history of anxious attachment leaves them with a deep need for affirmation and security. They fantasize about relationships in which all their needs are fulfilled: unconditional love, adoration, magical sex, constant reassurance. Meanwhile they are unconsciously expecting the opposite: scarcity, capriciousness, sole emotional responsibility, and ultimately being hurt and left. These two conflicting visions create the terrible illusion of a relationship that will deliver our heart's desire and snatch it away in a single stroke.

Disillusionment Practice will help the Transforming Person to let go of both the magical fantasies and expectations of doom, and to see their lovers clearly. Rid of these illusions, the Transforming Person is free to find deeper intimacy, better sex, and an honest joy between partners.

Before we get down to the brass tacks of Disillusionment Practice, we need to identify the illusions that must be dispelled. In this chapter we're going to confront the Goddess/Prince. The Goddess/Prince is *not* a real human being;

The Goddess/Prince is a construct in the Nice Person's mind

nor does it represent the power, beauty, and glory of women or men as a gender. The Goddess/Prince is a construct in the Nice Person's head—one that prevents him or her from clearly seeing potential lovers and partners as they truly are.

THE NICE PERSON AND THE GODDESS/PRINCE

We speak of the Prince because it conjures up the image of Prince Charming from the fairy tale, and so many women have been brought up with the idea that someday their prince will come and save them from everything that is sad and difficult in their lives. The Prince is an idealization of men in general, but is particularly activated when a Nice Girl is romantically focused on one man. For Nice Guys, the image of the Goddess is profound. It too is a subconscious idealization which is eventually projected on any woman with whom the Nice Guy is romantically interested.

Consider this Nice Guy example: Joe tells Sally, "Carl and I want to get away for a weekend." She says it would be great for him to do that, though the next three weekends are not convenient because of Angela's soccer match and other school activities, and she doesn't want him to schedule anything for later in the summer because of the kitchen remodel. Joe is frustrated and resentful, but doesn't acknowledge this to himself and acts agreeably toward her. He apologizes for overlooking the soccer match. On Friday, Sally informs him that her two best friends have invited her to go camping, and that it's really important for her to go. Joe affirms her autonomy, helps her pack, and kisses her goodbye. Secretly, he resents that she is going while also being relieved that she will be gone. When she returns, he helps her unpack and listens for two hours about her experiences and insights. Three days later, he tells her he too wants to get his weekend away. She asks him why he doesn't just do it. She says she is tired of his wimpiness and wishes he would take charge of his own life. He feels defensive, but internally agrees that she is much better at taking care of her own needs than he is. Joe apologizes for not being more assertive. He feels emasculated and hopeless.

Joe has a Goddess construct in his head. Sally says that the next three weekends are not convenient, but Joe isn't hearing Sally, he's hearing the Goddess. If he does not please her, or worse, if he defies her, she may deem him unworthy. Now we're squarely into Joe's anxious attachment. Unworthiness equals coldness equals no sex equals no love equals abandonment. So Joe chooses to sacrifice to the Goddess and not hang out with Carl.

Why does Joe feel emasculated about asking to go out? Because he's not discussing his options with Sally the woman (although Sally the woman may well be doing her part to keep up this Goddess act), he's groveling before the Goddess. She who holds all Joe's happiness must be approached carefully.

CLINGING TO THE GODDESS

Joe is clinging to the Goddess construct in his head. His fragile sense of self-worth rises and falls depending on what he gets from Sally. He cannot yet fully imagine what it might be like to be free of this dependency, to find the comfort he seeks from within himself. Here are some of the indicators of a Goddess/Prince construct:

Single

- Assigning exaggerated positive traits to a man or woman you don't know
- Focusing on the *fantasy* rather than the reality of a relationship with a man or woman you know superficially
- Abdicating responsibility when dating; leaving decisions up to your date under the guise of politeness

Partnered

- Reflexively ignoring your lover's bad behavior
- Indiscriminately agreeing with your partner's point of view, fighting her or his battles, and championing her or his causes
- Worrying constantly about what your partner thinks and feels

These signs can be exhibited in a vast range of behavior, depending on the severity of obsession with the Goddess/Prince construct. Imagine a woman "in love" with a man she has barely met, who plays out scenarios in her head about their happy life together, and eventually becomes angry when he does not return her unspoken and misguided affection. This is a Nice Girl with a Prince construct.

Love at first sight for Nice People is like social drinking for an alcoholic

What's so wrong with falling in love at first sight? Isn't that intoxicating feeling the privilege of all new lovers? Perhaps, but Nice People are prone to becoming obsessed with a new relationship. Love at first sight for Nice People is like social drinking for an alcoholic—they cannot afford to indulge themselves because instead of seeing an actual man or woman, a Nice Person sees a Goddess/Prince instead.

THE MACHINATIONS OF THE GODDESS/PRINCE

If a person has a Goddess/Prince construct inside of them, their fantasies or their silence can have destructive results. Here's a look at a common cycle of destructive mechanisms built into the Goddess/Prince construct on page 145.

This cycle is pervasive and very difficult to interrupt.

THE DESTRUCTIVE GODDESS/PRINCE

The harm caused by a Goddess/Prince construct can be devastating, anywhere from the inability to get a date, to sexual problems, to broken marriages.

- Generates high stress
- Corrodes self-esteem
- Impairs emotional healing
- Damages capacity for genuine intimacy
- Increases risk of infidelity

THE CYCLE OF DESTRUCTION

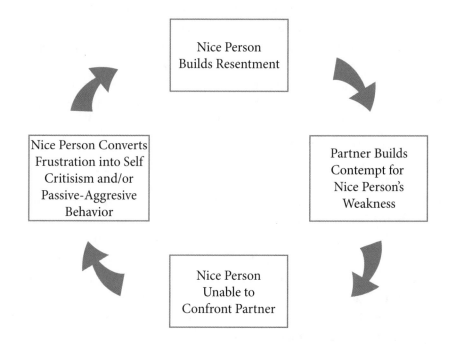

Day after day the Nice Person's habits—swallowing anger, over-apologizing, self-criticizing, self-deceiving when excusing a partner's behavior—take an extraordinary toll. Add to that the negative emotions that are evoked in a partner—impatience, judgment, coldness, scorn—and you've got a petri dish ripe for growing stress and low self-esteem.

Emotional healing is difficult for Nice People because their intense focus on the Goddess/Prince construct often leads to self-neglect. The man who works sixty-hour weeks, or neglects his health, or can't get together with the guys anymore, all in the name of his girlfriend or partner or wife, is a Nice Guy worshiping the Goddess construct. He may be unhappy, in pain, and unfulfilled, but that doesn't matter, as long as the Goddess shows him some signs of affection.

Healing from troubled or ending relationships becomes extremely challenging for Nice People because they are not just dealing with the potential loss of a lover; they are also trying to cope with the prospect of losing the Goddess/Prince. Nice People construct the Goddess/Prince to assuage their anxious attachment with the hope of getting the love they did not get as a child. So every time they go through a breakup with a lover, they feel abandoned all over again. This desperate feeling resides deep within their bones. No wonder Nice People often do desperate things when they are losing a partner. No wonder they don't believe their friends that say, "I know it hurts, but it's not the end of the world."

Intimacy

While Nice People have an intense craving for intimacy, they have a limited capacity for it. Nice People want to share closeness with a lover, but they are afraid to venture into the uncharted territory of complete honesty, which resides at the very heart of intimacy. Nice People are convinced that they cannot afford the dire risk of honesty because they believe it will threaten the Goddess/Prince. They are right. When the Nice Person sees the Goddess/Prince construct as it truly is, it will collapse. This is the beginning of disillusionment.

Nice People develop behavior that they hope will pass for intimacy—bringing home flowers, washing dishes, asking how their partner's day went, being an attentive lover. These are good things to do but they don't replace the loving honesty between two people that leads to trust and then to intimacy.

Intimacy is about honesty The Goddess/Prince construct makes honesty difficult on many levels, from life's little details to the most profound truths. Joe could have told Sally: "I really want to hear about your camping trip, but I've been hanging dry wall for the last four hours and I'm beat. Give me twenty minutes for a hot shower and then I'd love to hear everything that happened." But he didn't because he was anxious to appease the Goddess, and, two hours later, resentment is boiling up.

The Goddess/Prince construct works its same brand of nasty sorcery in the bedroom. If a person can't share honestly about sex with his or her partner for fear of upsetting the Goddess/Prince (and the bedroom can be one of the scariest places for Nice People), then intimacy becomes impossible.

Infidelity

Nice People are infidelity prone—both as perpetrators and victims—and the Goddess/Prince construct is the biggest reason. Add up the destructive effects we've been examining—high stress, corroded self-esteem, impaired emotional healing, and damaged capacity for intimacy—and it's not hard to see why. The last idea Nice People can entertain when they are desperately clinging to the Goddess/Prince is the possibility of being alone. And if the relationship is in tatters and the partner holds them in contempt and nobody's talking about it, it's a good guess that an infidelity train wreck is about to happen. If the compulsion is strong enough, the Nice Person may resort to seeking a new Goddess/Prince to replace the current one. Even more likely, the Nice Person's lover will convince themselves that it's okay to carry on a secret relationship that "meets their needs."

THE GODDESS/PRINCE TANGO

The unhealthy dance between Nice People and their Goddess/Prince begins even before the Nice Person meets a potential mate. When a Nice Girl finds a man who matches up with her unique pattern of yearning, she elevates him to Prince. As a part of this response, her natural danger alarms are suppressed and she has trouble seeing the man's flaws or weaknesses.

Let's look at one possible tango involving a Nice Girl:

Tammy Wants: A man who will appreciate everything she does for him—how she compliments him, how well she listens to him, how she pleases him in bed. Tammy wants to put Tre on a pedestal and worship him in return for the affection, fidelity, and reassurance she craves. She wants Tre to take care of her.

Tre Wants: A woman who will worship him, adore him, and idolize him. He also wants a woman who is smart, funny, sexy, and strong enough to make decisions for herself. At the same time, Tre is afraid of being dominated and needs to feel that he has control at all times.

Notice that some of the above wants are reasonable and healthy while others are not. It's when you put them all together that they become a recipe for disaster. At first these two get along quite well. She gets to worship, and he gets to be worshiped. She gets stroked for being such a great girlfriend. and he is constantly told how amazing he is. But sooner or later he wants to feel her backbone and all he gets is marshmallow. That's when he starts to lose respect.

The blame for this destructive dance is not always equally shared. A Nice Girl may meet a relatively healthy man, and if her Prince construct is strong enough she can eventually have him acting like a bastard. Similarly, a man with a powerful Goddess construct can turn a normally reasonable woman into a shrew. Nice People may be unconsciously terrified and/or enraged if their partner's love is not constantly turned on them, but they won't admit that anything is amiss. Or they may never make decisions, turning every responsibility over to their lover in the name of making them happy. Eventually, the Goddess turns into Goddesszilla and the Prince into the worst sort of frog.

On the other hand, Nice People often choose domineering partners who may not want to participate in ending the destructive cycle. In the sample tango above, Tre is probably not a good choice for a partner. Even if Tammy becomes a Transforming Woman, Tre will likely confuse her strength with dominance and her vulnerability with wimpiness.

KILLING THE GODDESS/PRINCE CONSTRUCT

Disillusionment Practice means rooting out, dissolving, and mourning the deeply held belief system of the Goddess/Prince construct. Here is a list of methods for disillusionment, followed by an explanation of each:

- Confronting the desperate belief that the love of the Goddess/Prince will fulfill you
- Attending to words
- Practicing vigilance
- Hearing your own voice

- Choosing reliance on yourself over dependence on the Goddess/Prince
- Trying it on
- Practicing grace

Desperate Belief

At the root of the Goddess/Prince construct lies the desperate belief that appeasing the Goddess/Prince will result in fulfillment. This is the big distortion.

In this context, there is no such thing as a One True Love or Heaven-Sent Destiny. No man or woman will ever complete us. This is a task only we can accomplish. We may have help from women and men along the way— friends, lovers, spouses, therapists, teachers—but the task of fulfillment is ours alone.

This truth is hard to take in. At first our hearts deny it, drawing our thoughts back into their old patterns: "If I'm nice enough, he (or she) will give me everything I need." We must remind ourselves over and over that no man or woman will ever fill the empty place in our heart.

No man or woman will ever fill the empty place in your heart

Practicing Vigilance

Awareness is the primary tool of Disillusionment Practice. Once Transforming People begin to recognize the Goddess/Prince thoughts, they must remain vigilant—remember, the thoughts come back from the dead. After all, Nice People have clung to their Goddess/Prince construct since early childhood, and it permeates every part of their lives. This is going to be harder than giving up chocolate or pornography or cigarettes or romance novels because the Goddess/Prince resides inside the Nice Person's own mind and heart. The Goddess/Prince may even be the thing that makes getting up in the morning seem worthwhile—"maybe today I'll meet my soul mate!"

Every time the Goddess/Prince thoughts return, we bring them into the light of awareness, leading us to the emotions underneath. With vigilance, the clingy Goddess/Prince thoughts and emotions return less frequently and with less power.

Hearing Your Own Voice

When the Goddess/Prince begins to fade, Transforming People come to rely more on themselves. This can be an exciting proposition. A Transforming Person, listening to their inner voice for the first time, may learn all manner of things. A man may realize he has a certain taste in clothing, or a woman may realize that she has a need to spend time alone, or they both may realize that their life goals shouldn't always take a back seat to their marriage.

> **One of the joys of being a Transforming Person is experiencing the solid masculinity or grounded femininity of knowing what you want independent of a partner's needs**

Hearing that true voice takes time and a combination of several practices: Awareness Practice, because the better we get at identifying Nice Person thoughts, the more clearly our own true voice can be heard; Brotherhood and Sisterhood Practice, because our own voice can be uncertain at first, and it helps to check in with trusted friends; Desert Practice, because perhaps for the first time we are acting as our own advocates; and finally, Warrior Practice, because relying on ourselves can be frightening and requires perseverance.

Trying It On

For Nice People, especially in relationships, it is hard to imagine the feeling of being free from the Goddess/Prince. In Warrior Practice we used the example of the baseball player trying out a new swing to improve, even though it is uncomfortable. In the following scenario, Chelsea "tries on" self-reliance.

Chelsea wants to get her PhD and pursue her dream of teaching mathematics at a university. Her husband, Dan, has offered some verbal encouragement, but continues to rely on her financially while he struggles to make a living as a musician.

Chelsea says to Dan, "I want to have a planning session about my grad program." Dan says, "Sure, maybe sometime this weekend." Ordinarily, this is where this conversation would fizzle, and Chelsea would walk away hurt and frustrated, knowing that the weekend session will never materialize.

Here's the moment for Chelsea to act like she relies on herself. She says, "No, Dan, we always say that and never get around to planning. We have time right now, and I want you to do this with me." Dan says, "Can't this wait until later? I wanted us to watch a movie tonight." But Chelsea perseveres. She says, "This is too important to me to keep putting off. I want you to sit with me and work out this plan."

When Chelsea says this, she may be acting very casual, like it's no big deal. But she's spent five years with Joe (and twenty-seven years with her own Prince construct), and, for the first time, she's going to take a stance. This *is* a big deal. This is uncomfortable. This does not feel natural. But Chelsea does it anyway. Probably, Dan will see through her casualness. It is entirely possible, however, that he'll also be impressed with her stance, even secretly enjoying her show of gumption, and sit down to talk. Or he may test her further to see how strong her resolve is. After all, Dan is just as used to getting his way as Chelsea is with giving up hers. But Chelsea quietly persists until they sit down and talk.

Chelsea is faking it here. She's practicing self-reliance until she really feels self-reliant. The more she does it, the more she will get used to it. Eventually Chelsea will not even have to gear herself up for this kind of conversation because she will expect to get her needs met.

Dan too will get used to this idea and expect Chelsea to take care of her own needs. In fact, he will eventually find it an enormous relief. No longer does he feel vaguely guilty about not making Chelsea happy because she takes care of that herself. He even discovers that he can raise an objection to Chelsea's plans and that she will honestly consider his opinion and still take care of herself. No more hidden resentment!

Another possibility is that the conversation may not go so smoothly. Maybe Chelsea is all geared up for a fight and doesn't give Dan the time he needs to get used to this new behavior. Like a batter changing her grip, maybe the first time up she gets frustrated and swings wildly. Chelsea cuts off Dan's objections and states angrily that she needs to talk right now and he can just damn well deal with it! Remember that Nice People are full of suppressed anger, and when they start expressing it, they can be unskillful at first.

There are other reasons that an argument might ensue when Chelsea stands up for herself. Maybe Dan got into a relationship with Chelsea precisely because he needs to always be the focus of attention. Perhaps he will never get used to or enjoy Chelsea's emerging self-reliance. In this case, Chelsea has a hard road in front of her, which may include reconsidering her relationship. This is a terribly difficult decision, but it is one of the possible destinations on the road to transformation.

One last point about Dan and Chelsea. In the example, Chelsea acts without letting Dan know what she is up to. That can be okay at times. But in a good partnership, the work of transformation can be shared. In this case, Dan and Chelsea would have already spoken about her process of transformation. In the early stages it may be appropriate for the Transforming Person to overtly tell their partner that they are "taking a stand." As the transformation moves along, it will be understood between the couple that the work is going on underneath their negotiations.

Practicing Grace

In Sisterhood and Brotherhood Practice we talked about the need for extending and receiving grace from friends. Grace is equally important to Disillusionment Practice, not only for our partner, but for ourselves. Couples learning a new way of relating might as well be learning ice dancing when neither one can skate. There will be a lot of falling down and maybe some bruising. To pick themselves up and continue the dance will require patience, forgiveness, and a sense of humor.

MOURNING THE GODDESS

In Desert Practice we discussed in depth the emotions that are stirred up with the rising awareness of being a Nice Person. Fear, anger, sadness—all may raise their heads in this awakening. So too may contentment, triumph, and joy be stirred. But if Desert Practice was a stick to stir things up, then Disillusionment Practice is like taking that stick and whacking a hornet's nest. The emotions are powerful because when the Goddess/Prince dies, it must be grieved.

When Transforming People accept in their heart of hearts that no Prince or Goddess is coming to make their life better, they are likely to experience feelings ranging from relief to guilt to joy to grief. All of the practices we have been learning will be required to weather this emotional storm: Awareness Practice to be mindful of the feelings; Desert Practice to cre-

Take good care of yourself when you are grieving for the death of the Goddess/Prince

ate a time and place to experience the feelings; Warrior Practice to hold the emotions; Brotherhood/Sisterhood Practice to give us support; and Family Practice to help us understand the source of the emotions.

It is also important that we not be relentless about experiencing the death of the Goddess/Prince. There is a tendency amongst Nice People to grind their own noses in their grief, to punish themselves for having created the illusion in the first place. Part of Awareness Practice is noticing when the emotions become overwhelming. It is important to take care of ourselves, even escape for a while if it feels good: exercise, watch a good movie, meditate, kick back and read the paper, etc.

Nevertheless, there are good reasons for experiencing, as much as possible, the feelings associated with the death of the Goddess/Prince. When a Goddess or Prince is buried and properly mourned, its burial ground becomes incredibly fertile soil in the Transforming Person's heart. Relationships that spring from this soil grow stronger, more flexible, and more vibrant.

A DIFFERENT KIND OF LOVE—REAL WOMEN AND REAL MEN

Seeing the Lover Clearly

As Disillusionment Practice takes hold and the Goddess/Prince construct dies, Transforming People begin to see dates, lovers, and partners more clearly. This can be a jarring experience. Nice People have been wearing a pair of rose-colored glasses all their lives. Once they take off those glasses, that cute thing that she does where she's always late to everything and he has to make excuses might not be so cute any more. Or she may realize that his

Is he or she meeting me?

mean streak really does hurt, that it isn't getting any better, and that it makes him unattractive to her. Or he may realize that no matter *how* nice he is there is not going to be more sex.

Nice People are used to asking questions like: What else can I do for my lover? How can I help them out? Should I buy them roses before I get home . . . again? There's nothing wrong with these questions. But the Transforming Person needs to also ask the questions: "Are they giving to me as well? Do they reciprocate my respect and esteem?"

If the answer to these questions is "No," then the next questions will be "Are they *willing* to change?" and "Are they *able* to change?" Finding this out requires more than simply asking. These are questions that will take time and courage, requiring negotiations and ongoing dialogue to answer. It is possible that Transforming People may find that they are living with or married to a person who is harming them and has no intention of changing.

To see a lover clearly, we must first see ourselves clearly, recognizing both our own neediness and our anger. Here the rose-colored glasses analogy breaks down because the emotions that filter a person's judgment can't be popped off like a pair of spectacles. Rather, we must accept that we have filters, learn all we can about them, and make adjustments accordingly.

Seeing That Transcends

Fortunately, seeing clearly does not just lead to sad revelations of a partner's flaws. The Goddess/Prince construct also prevents us from seeing the true delights of a real woman or man. A Transforming Woman, for instance, may owe her boyfriend a big apology for all the times she has stuck him up on a pedestal. For whether she is adoring the self-generated image she projects on to him, or she is secretly resenting him for not living up to the Prince standard, she is still not seeing him for who he actually is. She may have the best partner in the world, but she can't truly see his worth until she sees him clearly.

When the veil is lifted, a man may find himself in the presence of a real woman who takes his breath away. Both her flaws and attributes are becoming steeped in meaning and therefore more precious. Perhaps his wife has a scar. Is the scar in and of itself beautiful? Aesthetically, perhaps not. Does the scar set the rest of her skin off exquisitely? Yes. A scar is a reminder of pain, of survival, and of experience. A Transforming Person is ready to appreciate the depths of meaning.

The Dark Side

Everyone has a dark side, a place where hurt and fear has created pettiness or vindictiveness or insecurity or any other character trait that causes harm to ourselves or those around us. Nice People compulsively hide their dark side. The problem is not that our dark side is bad; it's that we hate our darkness.

Strangely, the process of examining the dark side calls forth the very traits we want to cultivate. The act of scrutinizing and accepting vindictiveness or wimpiness or anxiety cultivates forgiveness and strength and calm. Instead of hating their darkness or hiding from it, Transforming People can see it clearly for what it is—a very hurt place inside of themselves. This hurt needs to be sponsored, like a hurt child who needs an adult to take her under wing, to hang out with her, play games, tell jokes, in short, to love her. When we develop compassion for our darkness, our transformation accelerates correspondingly.

A lover or partner is no different. When we practice disillusionment, we are also coming to know our partner's darkness. But we are warriors now, trained to face difficult emotions and understand separateness. We realize our emotions are our own and that our partner's emotions belong to them.

There is a searing beauty in a person's struggle with their darkness when they are in the process of transformation. There will be times that we fail in our efforts and times that we triumph. The difference between how we see our partners with and without the Goddess/Prince construct is like the difference between painting and staining a piece of wood furniture. Paint is intended to conceal the wood; stain is intended to reveal its character.

WORKING IT OUT

For Disillusionment Practice, we highly recommend the following:
- Conscious work with your partner. If you're in a relationship, tell them: "Okay, I'm going to work on this and I'd like your support."
- Meditation.
- Body work (acupuncture, martial arts, and yoga, as well as any sport or fitness program). Anxiety and the Goddess/Prince construct reside not just in your head and heart, but in your body as well.
- Therapy. There is no better, safer place to practice disillusionment.

Consider keeping a journal or notebook. Jot down everything and anything that has to do with the Goddess/Prince construct. Give the thing a title if you're so inclined: "Journal of Change" or "Goddess-Be-Gone" or "Frogs Only." This journal might include conversations or incidents in which you felt completely controlled by the Goddess/Prince construct or, conversely, in which you acted like a Transforming Person. You might note how you felt about such incidents; the shame or pride or compassion or anger. A journal is a good place for noting revelations and insights. A journal is also useful for time traveling—going back a year, reading some entries and saying: "Wow, I used to worship the Goddess/Prince, and now I'm starting to get free."

A NEW LIFE

More than anything else, Disillusionment Practice releases Transforming People from a host of anxieties. As the Goddess/Prince construct dies, the Transforming Person no longer needs to conform to a lover's world, and the rest of their life opens up. Like a groundhog poking its head out of the ground and blinking at the sunlight, the Transforming Person looks around and asks, what happens now?

As we discussed in Desert Practice, pleasant emotions that were once scarce will start popping up with startling regularity and at odd times. Disillusionment Practice intensifies this phenomenon. Happiness surfaces in the middle of loneliness. For former Nice People, it can be quite a new experience to feel content. As anxiety melts, so does self-doubt, and the Transforming Person will find themselves saying and doing things that would formerly have been unimaginable. Later, they will think, "I just stood up for myself, and it didn't feel weird, and I wasn't even angry about it."

Ironically, passion blooms like a prize flower in the fertile ground of disillusionment. Without the overbearing presence of the Goddess/Prince, the Transforming Person is free to love without anxiety and guilt. Sex becomes sweeter, lighter, funnier, and much more personal. Rid of anxiety, which acts as a short circuit in a person's communication system, the head, the heart, and the body are finally allowed to commune. Another blossom that thrives on disillusionment, perhaps less vivid than passion but more rare and delicate, is intimacy.

INTEGRATION

Disillusionment is the sixth of the seven practices, and although we have written about them in a particular order, they can be worked on simultaneously or one at a time. Integration Practice, up next, is about mixing these heady components into the exquisite brew that is the life of a Transforming Person.

10

Integration Practice

Individuality is only possible if it unfolds from wholeness.
—DAVID BOHM, PHYSICIST AND PHILOSOPHER

Jason is a man in his forties who, after decades of being a couch potato, decided to dedicate himself to being fit and healthy. At first he had only clues as to how he might accomplish this. He knew that he needed to lose weight and develop his strength and endurance. He knew that he'd been eating foods that weren't so good for him. He knew he didn't get enough sleep. His initial efforts weren't very successful—a fad diet dropped twelve pounds that were soon regained, and his attempt to complete a seventy-mile bike trek left him more in pain than in shape.

But Jason has persisted, and the longer he has pursued his goal the more effective he has become. Jason has been learning that health is a lifestyle. He has learned that his transformation comes from something more than a collection of techniques. It flows from a change of heart and mind. Jason's health practices—eating, exercising, stretching, resting, playing—are coalescing into a new way of being. Jason is becoming integrated.

So it is for Transforming People. By applying the practices in this book, we are each moving toward a personal integration, a "whole" that is greater than the sum of its parts. Integration Practice provides a way to bring the first six practices into alignment, facilitating a more seamless coordination of the practices within the events of everyday life.

To an extent, integration is a natural result of the practice of technique. Whether we are repeating scales on the piano, stumbling through the classic positions of ballet, or studying the syntax of a foreign language, we find that our awkward struggle eventually gives way to a greater fluency.

But Transforming Men and Women need more than mere repetition to fully realize the potential of the practices; integration must become a practice in its own right. We need the practices to melt into the psyche, where our intuition can apply them more deftly and spontaneously. Integration Practice facilitates that melting process and reinforces the bridge between the intuition and the conscious mind.

Integration Practice uses two different methods of bringing the practices together. Each method allows the Transforming Person to view the complex dynamics from both aerial and ground level perspectives. The first method emphasizes the dynamic interplay between the practices; the second focuses on a way to utilize everyday life experiences as the raw material for transformation.

INTEGRATION METHOD ONE: THE INTERPLAY OF PRACTICES

The first six practices may appear at first to be discrete processes that fulfill entirely separate functions, but in fact, each relies upon the efficacy of the others. This mutual dependency does not hinder the usefulness of a practice— it *strengthens* it. The web that is created by the interplay between practices provides an internal healing network for the Transforming Person. Integration Practice brings visibility and greater usefulness to this web.

Consider this update on Jason. His exercise regimen has now become better suited to his current level of fitness. He is learning about balanced nutrition and calories, and is steadily applying his new knowledge to his eating habits. He is drinking more water and less coffee. He is even uncovering old emotional connections to overeating and food.

Jason has been discovering how these practices operate in mutually supportive ways. Because he is doing more appropriate exercises, he is becoming more and more active, and since it isn't hurting him he is enjoying it greatly. Better nutrition gives him more energy for exercise and leaves him with fewer cravings, helping him to reduce his caloric intake. With less caffeine and more water coursing through his system, he is less prone to fatigue and chronic dehydration. His improved mood supports everything else. In three months Jason has lost just five pounds, but this time the weight is staying off, and Jason is feeling much better physically and emotionally. His life is changing, and he'll never go back to the way it once was.

Integration Is Attunement

What really makes Jason's long-term change successful is his attunement to the network of practices. Jason is able to adjust each particular habit to support the others. If his exercise intensity increases, he will also increase his mineral supplements and his water intake. If he goes through a stressful week, he is careful to pay attention to his stress level and the way that impacts his eating and sleeping habits. Integration Practice is about the development of this kind of attunement.

Now let's look at Daphne, a Transforming Woman who is learning to tune the various practices in her life. For years Daphne has juggled her career as a college professor with her domestic roles as wife and mother. In recent months, she has been confronting the causes and effects of her chronic niceness. Last week, she found herself sitting in angry silence as her husband criticized her for being too indulgent with their five-year-old daughter. In the past she would not even have realized that she was angry, but she has been learning to recognize her emotions (Awareness Practice) and has begun to understand that she stuffs her anger in the vain attempt to protect important relationships (Family Practice, Disillusionment Practice). Once she acknowledges her anger to herself, her old habit of being passive-aggressive becomes more visible as well, and she finds herself wanting to lash out at her husband—i.e., *active* aggression. But she has also been learning how to be present with her intense emotions without reflexively acting out (Warrior Practice). In this case, she recognizes her need to process her feelings and thoughts before taking them up with her husband. She tells him that she needs some time before talking more with him. To her surprise, her husband encourages her to do just that. For the next few days she carves out niches to walk and spend time alone (Desert Practice), bolstering that by getting extra time with a few close friends (Sisterhood Practice).

As Daphne reflects on how this particular episode has unfolded, she pays close attention to the ways in which the practices feed and support one another. She sees how her increased awareness enabled her to make different choices about how to respond to her husband's complaints. Her ability to restrain the urge to scream at him was strengthened by her confidence in other resources available within herself and from the handful of women that she has drawn close to her. Earlier in her work when she was focusing on Warrior Practice, she had often chosen to take the argument right back at her husband. This usually yielded a good result in the end, but with quite a bit of pain and upset on the way. Now, she is feeling a greater sense of partner-ship with her husband (even during conflict!) and is learning that this is partly because of her ability to reveal more of her feelings to him, combined with his increasing trust that she will accept ultimate responsibility for her own needs.

By studying how the different practices are coming into play, Daphne is reinforcing her attunement. She is able to access a more global view of what is happening at any given time, and her increasing consciousness is helping her to become more skillful at finding the most effective tool for the situation.

This method of Integration Practice is a bit like the scientific study of an ecosystem. A marine biologist might examine a region of shoreline, con-stantly alternating his vision from the micro level (for instance, evaluating the effects of temperature on plankton) to the macro level (looking at how the population changes in plankton affect the entire marine ecosystem). Likewise, we need to oscillate between the micro level (Daphne noticing that she is suppressing her anger) to the macro level (Daphne recognizing different ways that suppressed anger is an important theme in her transformation work). By moving back and forth between the micro and macro views, we are practicing integration.

INTEGRATION METHOD TWO: LIFE AS WORKSHOP

People often don't realize that transformational experiences can be found and cultivated from the raw material of daily life and can be invoked at any time. With intentionality, it is possible to develop a "laboratory for change" that unifies the disparate segments of life. Any life experience can be conceived of as an experiment in the transformation of thoughts, feelings, and behavior.

This "Life as Workshop" approach is an alternative to the conventional way of thinking that regards everything as being either good or bad, succeeding or failing, desirable or undesirable, superior or inferior. Instead, the Workshop approach regards *every* experience as an opportunity to grow and learn. Every event in your life—eating lunch, riding the bus, getting fired, making love, losing a friend, etc.—holds the potential to become an exercise that moves you forward on the path of transformation. It becomes, essentially, Lunch as Workshop, Commute as Workshop, Job Loss as Workshop, Sex as Workshop, and so on.

The ability to revisit an experience and see it as an experiment brings a new perspective to old problems. Indeed, what we think of as a "problem" begins to appear as something more like a portal—a passageway to something greater. Any difficult situation can initiate a journey that leads to discovery.

Components of a Good Laboratory

Every experiment is helped or hindered by the quality of the laboratory environment. A well-designed workbench and the right collection of tools can bring precision and quality to any endeavor; conversely, dirty beakers, miscalibrated machinery, and insufficient lighting can undermine the most well-intentioned efforts. For this laboratory, the right equipment includes a set of mature attitudes, supportive relationships, and invaluable resources.

ATTITUDES

One of the fundamental lessons that is taught to young athletes is that the body tends to follow the head; if you can control where your head is going, you will have much better control over your entire body. For Transforming People, a similar principle applies; our attitudes determine the usefulness of our work.

The willingness to change. We may think of ourselves as being willing to change, but sometimes that view is more about the past than the present and future: "I am in favor of the change that already took place in my life. Now I'd like everything else to change so that I can stay the way I am." *Willingness to change* is a psychotherapy cliché for a good reason—it often separates the path of healing from the path of "more of the same."

The willingness to accept responsibility for your own life. Regardless of who did what to bring you to this place in your life, it is now your job to take it from here. This attitude is a cornerstone of maturity and is indispensable in pursuit of true freedom and contentment.

The willingness to leave bad relationships. When a relationship (any relationship) is not good for you, there are only two healthy choices: either both people commit to making the relationship healthy, or you give it up. It can be complicated and emotionally difficult to evaluate a relationship; it can be even harder to know how to end one.

Four other attitudes round out the list:

- Life is rich with learning opportunities.
- Transformation is an ongoing lifestyle, and not merely a collection of techniques.
- Practice compassion toward self and others.
- Practice nonjudgmental awareness in all facets of life.

These eight attitudes infuse the Workshop approach with a positive energy that is grounded in reality. They emphasize the value of allowing things to unfold over time, rather than going for the quick fix. They embrace a perspective that there is an abundance of time, an abundance of goodness, and an abundance of opportunity.

RELATIONSHIPS

When considering the components of a good laboratory for change, relationships are crucial:

- The Sisterhood and Brotherhood provide support, encouragement, and mirroring. When we're lost in the woods, we need our brothers and sisters to help us see both the forest and the trees.
- If you are in a romantic relationship, it is critical that your partner be supportive of your transformation. If your partner is unable or unwilling to be an integral part of making life a laboratory, the work is extremely difficult and can be frequently sidetracked. If, on the other hand, there is a sense of partnership around this work, every facet of it is enhanced.

RESOURCES FOR DEVELOPMENT

Just as there are thousands of tools and gadgets that might be part of a home workbench, there is a tremendous variety of possible resources for personal development that can be included in your laboratory for change. We have listed several categories below, but we encourage you to continue to discover and add your own. Initially these resources are likely to come from places that are familiar to you, for instance, if you belong to a particular religion or civic group. Eventually it is important to branch out and draw from different mindsets and traditions. Keep in mind that this laboratory is intended to undergo periodic renovation; adding new tools and letting go of the old ones is a part of the process.

RESOURCES FOR DEVELOPMENT
- Teachers
- Mentors
- Therapists
- Books, courses, clinics, workshops, retreats
- Groups (men's/women's, recovery/twelve-step, therapy, spiritual, etc.)

INTEGRITY AND INTEGRATION

The Latin root *integer* is often translated as meaning "whole" or "complete." The word implies a sense of congruence, of being undiminished and uncompromised. *Integer* is the basis for the word "integrity," and indicates a meaning that goes well beyond the concept of simple honesty. The ancients understood that integrity requires a process of integration, a continual development of the connections between thoughts, feelings, and behavior. In this sense, Integration Practice is about the development of integrity—an internal sense of harmony.

Each of the practices we describe in this book are designed to engage the mind, heart, and body. When those three dimensions are in sync, the Transforming Person has access to a profound experience of connectedness to both self and others. This feeling of connectedness is the antidote to anxious attachment, and provides the Transforming Person with the way to feel whole within themselves while also finding a satisfying communion with their loved ones.

Section Three:
Romantic
Relationships

Before embarking on Section Three, it is worth taking a moment to pause and consider the remarkable changes in attitude that a Transforming Person brings to a relationship. While the 7 Practices are the work of a lifetime, positive change can be felt very quickly. As a Transforming Person you are:

- Developing a place of beauty and resource within—an expansive feeling of being okay—that is separate from your partner
- Increasing capacity for tolerating unresolved feelings, allowing for the timely exploration and resolution of conflict
- Learning to direct longing toward yourself, your spiritual practice, and your friends and family, rather than focusing it all on a lover
- Strengthening the body through healthy emotional practice, and the emotional system through healthy physical practice
- Recognizing the difference between healthy needs and obsessive cravings
- Developing resilience, which originates from a capacity for self-validation and is supported by clear and incisive mirroring from the Sisterhood and Brotherhood

- Accepting of the cycles of intimacy and separateness that naturally occur in a relationship (not obsessively pursuing merger)
- Embracing the need for intimacy, love, and sex, and welcoming those of a partner.

Transformation takes time. Some of the practices will be as uncomfortable as an ill-fitting shirt, while others slip right on as if they were tailored for us. As time goes on, it is often the difficult practices that make the biggest differences in our lives.

There will be times when we feel as if we are getting nowhere. But then along comes a sudden breakthrough, and we find ourselves acting with incredible compassion and conviction, as if we were someone else—someone we have always wanted to be. There will also be dramatic swings when we are anxious and self-doubting one instant and calm and confident the very next. This pendulum is a sign of change, and we can take heart by enjoying our bold, separate self, and storing the memory of what it feels like to have less anxiety.

The very fact that Transforming People are working on themselves is a rare and desirable quality in a relationship. Imagine going on dates with the confidence that Warrior Practice brings. Imagine starting a new relationship with the clear eyes of Disillusionment Practice. Imagine a long-term relationship gaining the respect and intimacy that only Awareness Practice can bring.

It is good and healthy to desire romance, but as Nice People our picture of romance was distorted by anxious attachment. The 7 Practices are a method for retraining our ourselves to give and receive genuine and nourishing love. Section Three brings the Transforming Person to a new kind of romantic relationship.

11

The Transforming Relationship

If you're dying to work on something, work on yourself. Grow yourself up and your relationship will change. Primary relationships are people-growing processes...Stop working on your relationship and realize that your relationship is working on you.

—DR. DAVID SCHNARCH,
AUTHOR OF *PASSIONATE MARRIAGE*

SIERRA AND KYLE

Sierra and Kyle are approaching their ten-year anniversary. Much has changed since the early months of their courtship when he was tossing pizza dough and she was apprenticing with a landscaper. Kyle, now managing a bookstore, has continued to share his love of the outdoors with Sierra, who has her own landscaping business. Most weekends they head for the mountains with bikes, kayaks, or skis, depending on mood and season. They are still a few years away from bringing a child or two into their fold, but they are laying the groundwork for that future.

What has changed the most, however, has been the inner workings of themselves and their relationship. Sierra is a Transforming Woman, having spent much of her life (and the early part of this relationship) being anxious to please. Kyle isn't particularly drawn to emotional work. However, as Sierra made changes to herself and the way that she acted in the relationship, he began to realize that he needed to make some shifts himself, if only to keep up with her. An interest in the martial arts led him to Aikido, then to the study of meditation with some exploration of Eastern philosophy.

Kyle and Sierra each bring their own backgrounds and current practices into the dynamics of their relationship. Sometimes they don't quite see eye-to-eye—Sierra gets frustrated at Kyle's analytical way of talking about matters of the heart, and Kyle sometimes feels put off by Sierra's "touchy-feely" lingo. But beyond the personal journeys that each are taking in pursuit of growth and happiness, they are discovering that something else is happening—their relationship is transforming.

A BRIEF DEFINITION

A Transforming Relationship has particular features that make it different from other serious, long-term love relationships. The details of these distinctions will become clearer as we go, but for starters it is useful to know a few things that are unique about Transforming Relationships:

- **Transforming Relationships are true partnerships.** Partners work cooperatively to design and develop the relationship. Each person brings their own personality and assets and seeks to enhance those of their partner.
- **Transforming Relationships are growth-enhancing, positive places to be.** The couple shares the intention of creating a relationship that fosters growth and healing in each person and develops intimacy between partners.
- **Transforming Relationships embrace honesty, respect, and fairness.** What gives a relationship strength and endurance comes from how we treat each other. "True" love comes from an authenticity of action—the ability and willingness to exercise the highest ethic toward each other.

A Transforming Relationship is a relationship that is devoted to the transformation of both people, and it requires the commitment of both people toward that end. Many Transforming People have partners who aren't very interested in personal growth, or don't see much need for it to be a focus in the relationship. Other couples might be working on personal growth individually, but they aren't yet ready to take the partnership to that level.

But for those couples who are ready, a Transforming Relationship can be a revolutionary process. It provides a foundation that will see a couple through tough times and will set the stage for amazing intimacy. The relationship can become the home that supports a lifetime of incredible journeys.

THE TRANSFORMING PERSON NEEDS A PARTNER WHO IS ALSO DEVELOPING

We have already described how useful it can be for the Transforming Person to have a partner who shares the same key values and attitudes about change. In this chapter we are taking that point one step further: for a relationship to be transforming it needs *two* people who are actively working on their own personal process of growth.

It should be emphasized right away that we are *not* saying that both people have to be using the same approach. Indeed, it can be very good for the relationship for each person to be bringing a different perspective and/or sensibility. The important thing is that both people are working on themselves, and that both are bringing the benefits of that work to the relationship. The dynamic of mutual development is essential for several reasons:

- **It improves both people's development.** A proverb says that as iron sharpens iron, so does one person sharpen another. When both partners are lovingly bringing the benefits of their personal work to the relationship, there is a continual process of enhancing and deepening the work of each other.
- **It creates common ground.** When one partner is growing and the other partner is not, the effect is a sense of distance in the relationship, a loss

of common experience and meaning. It doesn't matter if each partner is following a different path; if they are both working on themselves they will find it easier to attune to one another.

- **It promotes balance.** Healthy relationships don't need to be symmetrical (e.g., both people have the same skills, the same likes and dislikes, etc.), but they do need to be balanced (e.g., my skills are valued as much as your skills). If only one person is involved in personal growth, their capacities for intimacy, intensity, and honesty may outpace the capacity of the partner.
- **It's a lot more fun.** The process of growth gives a person a broader foundation and a temperament that is more open and facile. When both partners are doing this, they will share a greater capacity for joy and contentment.

"But My Partner Isn't Doing It Like I Am..."

The support of your partner's process can include some reservations. It isn't necessary to pretend to agree with everything they believe or endorse everything they practice. The support just needs to be honest and respectful.

Conversely, if your partner isn't supporting you, it can feel lonely and even oppressive. When this is the situation, your growth may be greatly compromised. It can lead to contempt, at which point thought should be given to involving a couple's therapist. Contempt is one of the most corrosive elements in a relationship and, like a termite in the floorboards, should be dealt with as soon as discovered.

SUPPORTING THE PARTNER'S GROWTH

When a person can feel the enthusiastic support of their partner, their personal growth work receives a turbo boost. Personal work can evoke difficult emotions such as anger, sadness, humiliation, and longing. With the backing of the beloved, the hard times get easier and the breakthroughs sweeter.

The following are some specific ways to support your partner's development. Keep in mind that your first priority is to take care of your own needs.

WAYS TO SUPPORT A PARTNER'S PERSONAL GROWTH PROCESS

- **Be verbal.** Remind them that you're on their side. Tell them when you admire what they're doing. Offer stories about your own experiences.
- **Be quiet.** Be prepared to listen to them without interruption. Don't comment on their process unless there is the invitation to do so.
- **Be concrete.** Do something for them. Offer to watch the kids, make dinner, pick up the dry cleaning, wash the dishes—any of these actions can be something that makes it easier for your partner to get to therapy, go rafting, write in their journal, or have that hard confrontation with their father.
- **Be patient.** Change takes time. We all need the patient understanding from our loved ones as we go through our various stages of growth. This exercise of loving patience is one of the best investments we can make, paying dividends not only for our partners, but also for the trust and goodwill that it brings forth in the relationship.

INTIMACY, PRIVACY, AND DECEPTION

One of the popular concepts about relationships is that partners should tell each other everything and nothing should be held back. This basically translates to "intimacy versus privacy," with the idea that you can have one or the other, not both. This idea is 180-degrees wrong.

Every man, woman, and child on the planet needs to have a sense of privacy. Age affects this need—adults require quite a bit of privacy, babies almost none. The need for privacy is also affected by culture and family influences, as well as one's own unique internal wiring. Regardless, everyone needs privacy, if only in the solitude of their own minds.

People buying into the "intimacy vs. privacy" idea may sincerely (or at least overtly) try to "tell all" to their partner. But they invariably run into a fundamental problem: The psyche doesn't like being dragged out into the spotlight. It doesn't matter how much they trust their partner. If a person doesn't voluntarily withhold thoughts or feelings that they're not really ready to share, the psyche will take over and start hiding things. The result is that the person is either going to lie to the partner or they're going to lie to themselves.

Imagine the following scenario:

> Julie and her husband, Maurice, are driving home after seeing a movie about a married man who had an affair with another man. At one point, Julie asks, "Mo, have you ever wanted to have sex with another guy?" Maurice is uncomfortable talking about sex in general, and feels particular shame about a sexual encounter he'd had with a male friend when both were about sixteen. He stammers and feels a little panicky. He doesn't really want to tell Julie about his homosexual experience and doesn't really even want to discuss his sexuality; yet, he also doesn't want to lie to her.

Maurice is in a pickle. He might lie to Julie and say that he's never felt that way; just as likely, he might say that he's never felt that way *and then convince himself that it's true.* Either way, his relationship would be undermined by deception, whether he's deceiving Julie or deceiving himself. The dilemma is created by the illusion that the only honest choice is to tell Julie everything that he thinks and feels. "Intimacy vs. privacy" is robbing them of both intimacy *and* privacy.

But Maurice has an option that protects his need for privacy while also being honest. He can tell Julie how he's feeling. It might sound like this:

"Wow, Julie, your question really shook me up. I need a little time to gather my thoughts."

Or, maybe like this:

"Julie, when you ask me that kind of question, about my sexuality and my history, I feel kind of threatened and I just want to clam up or say whatever I think will end the conversation. Maybe we can talk about something a little less loaded, and when I'm ready to tell you more about this stuff, I'll let you know."

The ball is now is Julie's court. She may respond defensively or insensitively to him. But let's imagine that Julie and Maurice are in a Transforming Relationship, and that they are committed to protecting each other's sense of privacy. Julie responds:

"Oh, I'm sorry Mo, I don't mean to intrude. Thanks for giving me a clear signal. So, maybe we could talk about finding some good dessert? I'm starving!"

Julie has backed off from her initial question, communicating an acceptance of Maurice. By changing the subject, she is helping both of them to shift gears in a loving and playful way.

Not all of these conversations will go this smoothly. Learning to incorporate privacy with intimacy can be challenging, particularly if that's not how you were raised. Fortunately, we don't have to be perfect—we just have to be persistent. The key in a Transforming Relationship is that both partners embrace the twin values of intimacy *and* privacy.

NO PENANCE FOR PREVIOUS GENERATIONS

Relationships are always affected by the past. Cultural heritage and family history permeate long-term relationships, and there is no escaping it. What we must decide is how to handle it.

Throughout human history, women have been hurt by men and men have been hurt by women. Many people have strong feelings about how they have been harmed, humiliated, or disadvantaged by members of the opposite sex. As a result, lots of women have difficulty trusting men and vice versa.

It is common, then, for Nice People in love relationships to try to make up for the damage done by other people of their own gender. A man might repeatedly apologize for the ways that men have been insensitive or violent, and may try to compensate by never challenging what his wife or girlfriend says, never permitting himself to shout or act angrily. A woman might repeatedly apologize for the ways that women have been manipulative or spiteful, and may try to compensate by always going along with what her husband or boyfriend wants, never arguing strenuously for her own needs. Often these acts of penitence are demanded by the partner, overtly or subtly, as though it is the job of the lover to make up for the disappointments and abuses of the past.

The Transforming Relationship calls for an end to all of this penance. We cannot erase the offenses that others have committed, and we cannot avoid reminding our partners of what previous men and women have done. Our challenge is to accept that our partner has been hurt, to offer them our best acknowledgement of that truth, but *not* to compensate for what others have done.

Henry and Martha have been dating for about a year. They are both in their early fifties, and among the things they have in common is that this is their first serious romance after painful divorces.

Martha, having spent twenty-one years enduring physical and emotional abuse from her husband, loves that Henry is a gentle man. She feels bitter about the long history of violence from men toward women and is sensitive about anything that reminds her of it.

In a recent conversation, Henry tells Martha about his love of college football—the intense rivalries, the fierce collisions, the "thrill of victory and the agony of defeat." Martha reacts with anger, asserting that football is a violent sport full of the typically male preoccupation with hurting people, dominating people, and humiliating the losers.

As a former Nice Guy, Henry feels the urge to downplay his interest in football and to assure Martha that he won't watch it on TV if she's around. But he realizes that this wouldn't really represent his true feelings, and that he would simply be trying to appease her fear and anger. In doing so, he would actually be respecting her less.

Instead, Henry focuses on the feelings Martha is expressing. He asks her to tell him more about what it is like when she encounters these male cultural elements. He asks her how it affects her feelings about him to know that he's a football fan. He does a lot of listening.

The next day, Martha asks him about the conversation and clarifies that she does not think of him as a violent man. She tells him that she struggles sometimes with the reality that he is male and that this can evoke fear and doubt for her. She also tells him how much she appreciates him talking to her about it. They both agree to keep the topic open, knowing that their feelings and perceptions will continue to evolve.

BEING DIRECT

A Transforming Relationship requires that both people be committed to a high level of honesty and openness. This in turn must be built upon a foundation of trust, creating an environment where two partners can feel safe enough to explore together the dark canyons and mysterious grottos of their minds and hearts.

Speaking with directness helps to build that trust; being indirect can undermine it. When a partner is direct with us, it helps us feel secure. We don't have to read between the lines, imagine what they are thinking, or guess what they are going to do next. When we are direct with our partners, it gives them the same benefits and enriches us as well.

Treat your partner with respect and compassion but not with kid gloves

Directness is something of an art form. On one side, we are attempting to be clear about something we are feeling or thinking; on the other side, we are considering the feelings of the other person. Being direct doesn't simply mean dumping whatever happens to be on our minds at the time. It isn't a license to be crass or brutal. The goal of directness is to create a bridge between partners that can carry meaning back and forth with clarity and loving kindness.

ACKNOWLEDGING ANXIOUS ATTACHMENT

The process of transformation can take a long time, and in the meantime, the anxiety continues to affect us and those with whom we are close. The fears, defensiveness, and troubling projections are likely to be confusing and disconcerting to a partner who doesn't know what's going on.

One of the features of people with anxious attachment is that they hate their chronic anxiety and often are compelled to hide it. However, there comes a time in a relationship when it is both important and appropriate for the Transforming Person to talk with their partner about their anxious attachment. This step can be a difficult one, requiring courage and sensitivity, but it also holds tremendous promise for deepening the relationship.

Consider how a person might handle the disclosure of other important conditions. For example, genital herpes becomes particularly relevant when a couple is about to become sexually involved; early-stage multiple sclerosis can have more implications for the future than for the immediate present; chronic depression can come into play at any time. Each of these conditions has its own set of features that impact the relationship; each has its own variables about the present and the future, as well as meanings

Disclosing your anxious attachment as soon as you meet someone probably won't feel good to either of you. It's an intimate topic loaded with vulnerability, and timing can really make a difference

for the person who has the condition. Anxious attachment, too, has its own set of features and personal relevance which must be considered when deciding when and how to disclose.

When to Disclose

In a romantic relationship emotions often get amplified quickly, like a small tropical storm building overnight into a ferocious hurricane. For a couple to manage these emotions, they need to be able to talk about them and explore their meanings.

It is important, then, to pay close attention to the ways in which your anxiety is affecting the relationship. If it's coming up on rare occasions and mostly takes the form of a few passing thoughts and feelings, it's probably not an urgent matter. On the other hand, if it's causing great distress and is having a significant effect on the relationship, it might be time to talk.

Consult your own feelings when thinking about this disclosure. It can be tremendously valuable to talk this through with a therapist or the Brotherhood/Sisterhood. It's okay to feel a bit nervous about it, but if you're feeling something more akin to a sense of dread, it may be an indication that you and/or your lover may not be ready to talk about this yet.

How to Disclose

Here are a few guidelines that can help point the way:

- **Stay in touch with your feelings.** Feelings are an important source of information. Pay attention to whatever emotions and body sensations you're having, and listen for what the other person says about their feelings as well.

- **Take your time.** Choose a time to talk when you can be unhurried, and allow for the likelihood that this is something you will revisit on occasion. There is time to get it right in the long run, so it behooves both of you to set aside any urgency and just let the conversation unfold at its own pace. If things get heated or scary, it can be a good idea to take a little break and come back to it later.

- **Do a dress rehearsal.** Make use of your Brotherhood/Sisterhood by asking one or two of them to help you prepare for this. This is not about writing a script—it's about thinking it through, deciding what are the salient points, and anticipating what questions your partner may have.

- **Allow plenty of room for your partner's questions and reactions.** It's easy to go into a conversation like this being preoccupied with what you want to say. But your partner will have their own concerns to talk about, and will need you to be able to hear them as well.

SEXUALITY IN THE TRANSFORMING RELATIONSHIP

Sexuality is at the center of a robust romantic partnership. Lovemaking can cross all terrains—physical, spiritual, intellectual, and emotional—invoking any and all of the senses. To infuse sex with courage, playfulness, and character is to open both body and soul to a universe of possibility; to allow sexuality to atrophy is to let something precious be wasted.

Me, You, and We

In a Transforming Relationship, the creation of vibrant sexuality is of great importance. As we have discussed in previous chapters, romance is a very tricky arena for Nice People, where the fears and fantasies of the anxiously attached child get played out in adult relationships.

But Transforming People are developing strengths that can make romance and sexuality highly satisfying and even transcendent. We are no longer anchoring our romantic/sexual experience in the pursuit of the Goddess or Prince; we are learning to be anchored within ourselves.

This sense of security allows us to go places romantically and sexually that we've never been before. Sexuality is all about the exploration of the boundaries between two people, the encounter of two beings in physical and spiritual dance, penetrating, receiving, and melting into one another with hearts and minds as well as bodies. When both people have a solid sense of themselves, they can progressively let down their guard, relax the "I" into the "we," and dwell for a time in a state of rapturous union. Paradoxically, when people are not well defined, it is very difficult to enter this state.

Putting the "I" Back in "Team"

Nice People can get preoccupied with satisfying their partner while neglecting their own experience ("I know it was good for you, but was it good for me?") Certainly it is great for lovers to be generous with each other but this *preoccupation* with the other ultimately dilutes the sexual experience—as though there are only one and a half people in bed, not two. The consequence for Nice People is that their sexual experience is dependent on their partner's intuition and generosity. Even a relationship that starts off with good chemistry eventually wilts in the wake of such passivity.

In the Transforming Relationship, each person accepts responsibility for their own sexual experience and satisfaction. They look to their lover as a resourceful partner, someone who will lovingly dance with them. There's no way around it—this means talking! Partners have to talk with each other about what they are feeling and thinking, what they want, what they'd like to try, what does and doesn't feel good.

THE TRANSFORMING RELATIONSHIP: THE BIG PICTURE

The fundamental nature of the Transforming Relationship is a mature interplay between separateness and connection. This relationship supports personal growth while also fostering deep intimacy, taking on the joyous responsibility of caring for three treasures—two individuals and one union.

The relationship formed by transforming partners serves as a kind of base camp for the adventures and trials yet to come. From this secure foundation, the couple can venture beyond their own frontiers—experimenting, testing, exploring, journeying—to create a life of great communion.

12

Creative Conflict

True love is the only just and holy war. Two friends pledge loyal opposition to one another. I vow that I will defend the integrity of my separate being and respect the integrity of your being. We will meet only as equals; I will present myself to you in the fullness of my being and will expect the same of you. I will not cower, apologize, or condescend. Our covenant will be to love one another justly and powerfully; to establish and cherish inviolable boundaries; to respect our separate sanctuaries. We will remain joined in the sweet agony of dialogue, the contest of conversation, the dialectic of love until we arrive at a synthesis.

—SAM KEEN, *FIRE IN THE BELLY*

WHY DOES CONFLICT SCARE US?

For anyone who has spent a lifetime being anxious to please, conflict is the enemy. It lurks in the shadow of every friendship and in the heart of every love affair. No matter how nice, how appeasing, or how careful the Nice Person is, conflict arises. And when it does, the Nice Person responds reflexively, the way a knee reacts to the explorative tap of the doctor's hammer. Reflexive actions may include: submitting, going silent, getting surly, or being even nicer. Later, there will be licking of wounds, shame, red-faced private anger, or perhaps some good old-fashioned passive-aggressive revenge.

What is conflict? Why must it necessarily arise? And why do Nice People fear it? In the opening quote Sam Keen says, "True love is the only just and holy war. Two friends pledge loyal opposition to one another." Is he saying that true love must involve conflict?

> **Done well, conflict can be the beating heart of a romance**

He is, and it does. The conundrum is that we are simultaneously individuals who are different from one another and mammals who need one another's company. Over and over, we seek one another out, and then our differences—our unique needs, opinions, ethics, chemistry, senses of humor, pleasures, and perversions—collide. Conflict, done badly (and it is often done badly), can sound the death knell of a relationship. Done well, it can be the beating heart of a romance.

SORE POINTS AND REFLEX

Nice People believe that their personality (i.e., their "niceness") is what makes them lovable. They can become highly defensive, then, when they are being confronted with the idea that they have not been considerate or that they have acted badly. Once a sore point is engaged, the reaction is swift. It may be to give up and weep; or it may be to snipe angrily from behind cover; or it may be to put up an impenetrable shield and hide. Whatever the mechanism, it was developed long ago, and now happens without the Nice Person thinking about it.

Now, multiply the difficulty by two because each partner has his or her own sore points. One person's reflexive action triggers another person's reflexive action like a pinball between two electronic bumpers. And the action is exponential, speeding up and increasing in intensity.

Let us assume for a moment that the partners in the following dialogue love each other and are a good match. Despite their compatibility, they argue often. In this argument, it is bedtime, and Dave has just returned to the bedroom from downstairs. Marjean has promised to lock the door but once again has forgotten. As the argument picks up steam, the same sore point is repeatedly struck in each of them: the fear of rejection. Notice how each statement is a defensive reflex that hits the other person on the sore point, evoking yet another reflex.

A NICE COUPLE CAUGHT IN A REFLEXIVE ARGUMENT

Marjean:	"Why did you go downstairs?"	She feels shame that she keeps forgetting to lock the door. Reflex: *Attack by intimating that he was snooping*
Dave:	"I was just turning out the lights."	He feels shame that she detected his secret agenda. He's afraid that she will attack him if he confirms it. Reflex: *Avoid the conflict by lying*
Marjean:	"I heard the lock turn."	She's afraid that he doesn't respect her and he won't admit it. Reflex: *Suggest that he is lying*
Dave:	"I went down to turn the lights off and I happened to notice the door wasn't locked. Are you saying I shouldn't lock the door at night? How dumb is that?"	Feeling more exposed. Hurt that she doesn't appreciate his urge to protect her. Reflex: *Continue to lie (petulantly); add a counterattack*
Marjean:	"I'm not dumb, I'm just not paranoid like you. What are you so afraid of?"	Afraid that her shortcomings are being exposed and that he will demean her. Reflex: *Purposely change the meaning of his words; attack his masculinity*
Dave:	I'm not afraid...you're like a little kid. I'm tired of taking care of you."	Afraid that she won't respect his masculinity. Hurt that she's not noticing his protective intentions. Reflex: *Deny; attack her sense of competence*
Marjean:	"I don't need you to take care of me. I did just fine without you, Mr. Macho."	Feeling more ashamed and hurt. Reflex: *Deny her vulnerability; threaten the relationship*

In seven quick sentences, this "Nice" couple has traveled from a concern about an unlocked door to questioning their relationship. It's a nasty ping-pong match, using reflexive action for paddles and the relationship as the battered ball. If they play this game regularly, their relationship may not last. Yet, it is evident that neither person is arguing about what really is in their hearts. So how do we stop the game? The first step is for the players to set down their paddles.

AWARENESS

Let's review the cycle of awareness:

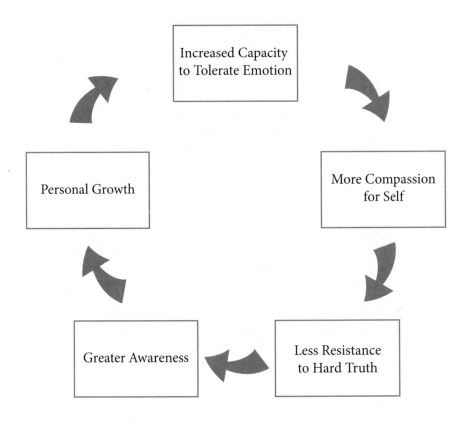

We're starting the cycle at "Increased Capacity to Tolerate Emotion" because reflexive reaction is caused by pressure on a person's sore points, and that pressure engages the basic fears of the anxiously attached.

Three steps to increasing the capacity to tolerate emotion:
1. Become aware that you have emotion
2. Examine your emotion
3. Develop compassion for your emotion

Relearning conflict is the process of bringing our emotions into the open and exposing them to the light of compassion.

REEDUCATING THE REFLEXES

Baring our emotions and developing compassion for ourselves is a counter-intuitive process and it requires Warrior skills. As we have seen, reflexive action started at a very young age to protect us from harm. But now, in adulthood, it is getting in our way.

Let's take previous the example. When Marjean realizes that Dave is downstairs, she gets mad and *then* she concludes that he is snooping. This may sound like a simple process, but in fact, a whole series of undetected thoughts and emotions have gone through Marjean. Notice, for instance, that Marjean justifies her anger by deciding that Dave is snooping; the anger leads to the thought, not the other way around. It is time to reeducate her reflex.

What happens if Marjean is practicing awareness? The moment she hears her husband downstairs, she feels her gut tighten and says to herself:

"Youch, my stomach feels tight and that means trouble. What is it? It's Dave downstairs, and I'm afraid he'll find out I forgot to lock the door again. Wow, my face is all flushed. I feel like I did when I was little and got yelled at for spilling my milk—ashamed, which makes me want to rebel. Now I'm feeling trapped and angry at Dave."

This is a Transforming Woman, a focused warrior with an active Awareness Practice. Marjean is actually able to witness the entire cascade of her emotions. As we have already discussed, this is an advanced state achieved after much practice. In the beginning, she may notice only one of these emotions or physical states, or she may notice them two weeks after the fact.

Marjean has taken two steps toward increasing her capacity to tolerate emotions; the first is to recognize that she's feeling something, and the second is to examine her feelings. She notices her body's response—tight stomach and flushed face. She makes associations, like noticing that her shame reminds her of when she was a little girl and spilled her milk. She then notices how that feeling of shame leads to feeling trapped, which is an old and profound fear of hers. She even notices the order in which her emotions and body sensations occur.

In order to achieve awareness, Marjean has to overcome a fear of the awareness itself. But once she does, she has the liberating experience of recognizing that her world has not fallen apart as she feared it would. In fact, successful awareness is often accompanied by a sense of enormous satisfaction. It is the Warrior's triumph at achieving a new level of skill.

Using Awareness Practice and Warrior Practice, Marjean has begun to reeducate her reflexes. She has increased her capacity to tolerate emotions, and developed a greater compassion for herself. She is now ready to move to the next level in her relationship.

SETTING UP CONFLICT

The way a couple sets up a conflict goes a long way to determining how creative the conflict will be. Together, the couple can:

- Vigorously protect an environment of safety and respect
- Notice sore points and interrupt reflexive actions
- Create the right environment for the conflict (time, place, structure)

Vigorously Protect an Environment of Safety and Respect

Conflict in our culture is presented as a contest of wills that must inevitably produce a winner and a loser. Not surprisingly, when conflict arises, our breathing gets shallow, we get a little sweaty, our heart rate goes up, and we steel ourselves for fight or flight. The idea of using conflict as a mutually creative process is (like reeducating our reflexes) counterintuitive. We do not come into the world knowing how to do creative conflict, nor are we trained to do it. Like any other skill, it takes time, practice, and a big dose of good humor before it becomes natural to us.

We do not come into the world knowing how to do creative conflict

In a way, creative conflict is similar to a staged fight in a movie. It looks like a fight, and there is real danger, but it is carefully set up to minimize the chances of getting hurt. The goal of a staged fight is not to produce a winner or loser, but to further the plot of the movie and illuminate the nature of the characters. What are the top three concerns of any good fight choreographer? Safety, safety, and safety.

SAFETY MEASURES TO REMEMBER IN CREATIVE CONFLICT:

- Respect your partner (even when angry)
- Tolerate your partner's intense emotion (without acting reflexively)
- Practice expressing intense feelings while not attacking
- Remember that hurt and anger are masking tenderness
- Allow your partner some separateness and sanctuary
- Be open to self-examination and change
- Be open to, and grateful for, your partner's change
- Allow differing views to coexist with love and respect

None of these stances are easy to cultivate, but if you are working with the 7 Practices, you have already touched on each of them. The goal now is to expand the practices outward to include your partner.

Notice Sore Points and Interrupt Reflexive Actions

Remember how the scenario unfolds: Dave goes downstairs and Marjean gets angry. She watches her body, thoughts, and feelings and realizes she's mad at Dave for checking up on her. But Marjean knows that she is probably part of the problem since she's got some Nice Girl in her and really does wish she could remember to lock the door. Nevertheless, she asks, "Why did you go downstairs?"

Dave can hear the potential conflict in her voice and feels his temper flare because he is tired of feeling like he can't trust her about the door. As he reflects on his thoughts and feelings, he notices:

- That he doesn't want her to think he's been checking up on her
- That he *has* been checking up on her
- That he doesn't want her mad at him
- That he doesn't want to lie to her

On top of all that, he's exhausted and knows he's bad at conflict when he's tired. At this point, Dave reviews his options before he speaks. Then he says: "Okay. I realize we've got to talk about this, but I don't want to do it now. I'm tired and I don't want to argue in bed. Could we talk about it tomorrow?"

This is a bold move. First, Dave's acknowledges that there *is* a conflict—a crucial step in the process. Then, he removes the ping-pong paddle from his own hand. Dave has observed his reflexive sore points and not acted on them.

But it takes two to tango. What will Marjean do?

Create the Right Environment for the Conflict (Time, Place, Structure)

Marjean recognizes that having a conflict when they are both tired is a recipe for disaster. Her experience also tells her that any conflict late at night makes for a lousy night's sleep and everyone wakes up madder the next day.

Even though she's still angry with Dave, she admires his restraint for not snapping back at her because she knows this is a tender subject for him as well. She says, "Okay. How about tomorrow after lunch? I'll meet you in the living room."

PHYSICAL SPACE

Let's stop for a moment to say a word about physical space. A couple needs to find a safe space to engage in conflict. Many couples will not have a conflict at the dinner table because they consider it bad for their health and digestion. For similar reasons, the bedroom is unfavorable because the bed is a place best reserved for peace and pleasure. Marjean chooses the living room because they are both comfortable there, because they can sit across from each other and have a little space between them or sit next to each other, and because it's easy to walk into the bedroom or kitchen if one of them needs to get away.

Now, mind you, both Dave and Marjean have been pretty carefully controlled about what they have said so far—they both sound a little stiff. That's because both of them have had their sore points touched and they're holding their emotions. Dave says, "That sounds good. Thanks, MJ. Tell you what, we only have an hour tomorrow. How about I just shut my trap and let you speak your piece? I'll listen to you and honor what you have to say. Then I'll take a day to let everything sink in and maybe on Wednesday—same place, same time—I can say what I need to say."

Dave just did several great things. First, he thanks Marjean for her restraint. Second, he calls her MJ, a signal of affection between them that is his way of saying, "I love you even if I'm mad at you." Then he proposes a structure for the conflict—he is going to just listen. If he can stick to it, Dave has not only taken away the ping-pong paddles, he's changed the entire game.

> **Conflict is a precious and delicate thing. Handle it as you would a baby, with reverence and gentle humor**

"Sounds good," Marjean says, and winks at Dave. "I know it's hard to live with someone who's right all the time." Now Marjean is being playful, but there is method to her madness. Having a sense of lightness can be crucial to good conflict as long as the intentions are clear. If the humor is meant to hide an emotion, mask a hurt, or take a quick jab, then it will be harmful. If it is meant to lighten the mood, acknowledge one's own flaws, or show that love is still present, then humor is a blessing.

ENGAGING IN CONFLICT

Dave and Marjean prefer to have a day or two before and between an argument, but some couples might find this maddening and want to engage more quickly. Even so, it is important to have some alone time in order to cool down, examine your emotions, and collect your thoughts. Each couple should develop their own special place and time for conflict.

At lunch, there has been some nervous joking between Dave and Marjean, including the suggestion that they each choose their weapons—Marjean opts for a dagger of "backstabbing" while Dave decides on the ever-popular "last word" club. But now the time has arrived. Remember, the title of this chapter is Creative Conflict and creativity is the name of the game.

ESSENTIAL SKILLS FOR CREATIVE CONFLICT INCLUDE:

1. Honoring the conflict and looking both ways before crossing the street
2. Speaking the truth
3. Expressing difficult and frightening emotions
4. Giving an authentic compliment
5. Holding two or more emotions at once
6. Receiving difficult and frightening emotions
7. Active listening
8. Responding

Honor the Conflict:
Look Both Ways before Crossing the Street

Before Marjean starts saying what's on her mind, she and Dave say a few words to honor the creative conflict they are entering into. This step allows the couple to acknowledge that they are about to do something important and difficult. It reminds them of the skills they will need in order to do the conflict well. It is a way to make sure that the couple looks both ways before crossing the street; that is, each person feels that they are ready and that the other person is also ready.

Each couple has their own particular way of honoring a conflict and they should develop a style that suits their tastes. It may be as simple as saying "I'm ready. Are you ready?" Or it might be calling upon God individually or together in mutual prayer. Or they might speak words honoring one another's humanity. Perhaps only one person wishes to speak and the other remains silent. As long as they are both honestly open to the possibility of truth and change, the words will work and the street will be safe to cross.

Marjean says: "I promise to speak my true feelings. I promise to look at my part. I promise to remember I love you and myself. I promise not to attack you." Dave speaks similar words about his intent to listen well. They have sanctified their conflict.

Speaking the Truth

Marjean has used her time wisely, finding a few moments in the morning to scribble a little list of what is bothering her.

Without apology she launches into her main complaints: she feels like she's being spied on; she doesn't think Dave trusts her; she feels like he sneaks around to check up on her; she feels like she's being treated like a child; she thinks he doesn't respect her intelligence; and she feels

When pointing out a problem she or he is having with a partner, the Nice Person has an urge to preface, sugar-coat, divert, and obfuscate

like Dave thinks she will not be safe without his maleness around to protect her.

Learn How to Express Difficult and Frightening Emotions

Talking about it brings back the feelings, and Marjean starts getting angry again. She says that when Dave treats her like a kid she just feels stifled and it makes her want to just walk out the door and not come back. She says she has noticed that when Dave talks to her about locking the door, he gets the same tone in his voice as when he talks to his fifteen-year-old daughter from his previous marriage. It feels like he's being "as-reasonable-as-possible-with-someone-who's-acting-like-a-child." And lastly, Marjean blurts out, she really, really, really can't stand it when he takes her beautiful cherry wood spoons and scrubs them with soap and a brush even after she has told him repeatedly that it will ruin them. It makes her feel like he doesn't listen to anything she says and doesn't value her and doesn't love her.

Marjean has stated her problems without apology or preamble. She has also allowed herself to feel her emotions without turning them on Dave.

TURNING ON A PARTNER MAY INCLUDE:

- Saying hurtful words
- Using sarcasm
- Diagnosing your partner ("It's the same issue you have with your mother.")
- Assigning your partner's motives ("You take that tone just to make me feel small.")
- Expressing emotions in a nonspecific way ("I hate you" as opposed to "I hate when you do this," or "When you do this it enrages me.")

TWO KEYS TO EXPRESSING DIFFICULT EMOTIONS:
1. Focus on your own feelings and problems
2. Keep a connection with your partner

Marjean has applied the first key by sticking to what she feels, thinks, and notices. She has used the second key by looking Dave in the eyes as she speaks. Watch what happens next.

Neither Marjean nor Dave speak for a bit. Finally, she looks up at him and has to stifle a giggle. "If I were you I'd be about to explode. How are you doing?"

Dave laughs and says, "This is hard, but I'm doing okay. I'm hearing you."

Even though Marjean is angry, she has the wherewithal to remember and acknowledge that this conflict is as difficult for Dave as it is for her. She says, "I really appreciate you listening to me. It helps a lot!"

Learn How to Give an Authentic Compliment

Ah, the compliment. It is such a simple gift to give, but so often overlooked. One compliment can change the course of an entire conflict—change it from a win/lose proposition to a risky, passionate show of love between two people. There is only one rule: The compliment must come from a place of honest gratitude. It doesn't work if it's manipulative, false, or forced. Put simply, when a person feels gratitude or affection or love in the middle of conflict, it helps to express it. In this case, when Marjean expresses her appreciation for Dave's good listening, she realizes that there are a few other things she appreciates about Dave. She says, "I've got to tell you that even though it makes me mad when I think you're treating me like I'm a kid, I do like that you want to protect me. I like that you care about my safety."

Holding Two or More Emotions at Once

Marjean is holding two emotions at the same time: She is angry, and she is appreciative. These are separate feelings that she can examine and feel depending on which one she turns her thoughts to. This ability becomes much easier when the desperation of the Nice Person has subsided through use of the 7 Practices.

Learn How to Receive Difficult and Frightening Emotions

It is time to find out how Dave is doing. As the receiver, it is Dave's job to be fully present with both his partner and himself. Learning to tolerate intense emotion within the partner sets a tone of acceptance and allows profound experiences of understanding and growth. However, we cannot stress enough that this is an advanced and difficult skill. People are not born knowing how to accept intense emotion with love, nor are they born knowing how to cope with the corresponding intense emotions that arise in themselves. In a moment we will look at the skills required for this task, but the first and foremost is compassion for self. The receiver must understand that it is natural to feel even the darkest emotions.

HERE IS A BRIEF SUMMARY OF MARJEAN'S MAIN COMPLAINTS:

- Thinks she's being spied on, feels like he sneaks around
- Dave gets tone of voice like he's speaking to a child
- Feels like he's being macho about protecting her
- Wants to walk out the door and not come back
- Ruining her cherry wood spoons means he doesn't love her

It's easy to imagine the range of reactions that Dave has to all of this. He is silent on the outside, but inside he may be feeling anger, outrage, embarrassment, guilt, annoyance, indignation, fear, or any combination thereof. So, how does he do it? How does Dave sit there and not reflexively strike back? Well, we're right back at the beginning—Dave has a great deal of internal space that allows him to feel strong emotions without reacting reflexively. Not only that, but he is aware that when Marjean speaks about her feelings they are not necessarily a reflection on him or their relationship.

When she says she wants to walk out the door and not come back, it doesn't mean that she is planning on doing so; it merely means that she felt like doing it. Dave has felt like walking out himself more than once. When he hears Marjean speak those words, he feels a fear of being left and simultaneously recognizes that he is not being left.

In conflict, a Transforming Person stands strong within themselves. They do not preempt the conflict by walking out the door or conversely by rolling over and exposing their belly

Active Listening

Dave's job is to establish a sense of connection with Marjean—to be present with her feelings and his own. This does not mean he is putting on a fake "listening" face and inwardly reviewing baseball statistics or trying to remember all the lyrics to "Bohemian Rhapsody." Dave is truly taking in what Marjean says, and she can see it in his eyes. There is no need for Dave to over-respond, nor does he need to hide his emotions. If something hurts, it hurts. If something makes him laugh, he will laugh. But Marjean can see by his body and face that he is acknowledging her.

Responding

The next day, Dave is feeling calmer. He has been able to sort through Marjean's words and he picks his battles.

- He acknowledges that he does check the door, but explains that he is concerned for their safety. Then, he admits that lately he's been checking up on her.
- Dave says that he didn't realize he was taking an authoritarian tone with Marjean. He apologizes and says that he will work on not acting like an authority figure.

- He says that sometimes he feels like she purposely acts childishly and forgets to lock the door when she's pissed off or wants something from him. He requests that she take a look at this possibility.
- Dave points out that he also sometimes feels protective toward her and that this is something he doesn't want to change.
- As for the spoons, Dave apologizes and says that he will develop a strategy for properly taking care of them.

Notice that Dave does not suggest any preemptive solutions—that is, a solution designed to squelch any further difficult feelings. When the time comes for solutions, both Dave and Marjean will have expressed their fears and concerns and will be much more likely to calmly pursue a practical resolution to the problems.

Notice also that Dave does not even address Marjean's worry that he doesn't love her because he doesn't properly clean her spoons. Dave knows that sometimes the act of expressing an emotion is sufficient and needs no response.

Often, it is enough for someone to speak their mind, and no response is necessary

Of course, this conflict might continue. Dave may well have some issues of his own to bring up. Or perhaps Marjean has made some discoveries about why she sometimes acts irresponsibly. Dave and Marjean might do several more rounds of talking and listening, or they might just finish with a discussion. At this point, their emotions are no longer out of control and they have each honored the other with frank disclosure and receptive listening.

THE HARD PARTS

Dave and Marjean are fictional characters, and it's easy for the authors to engineer positive conflict as an example. But reflexive defenses are ingrained, and couples may repeat painful patterns of behavior, wearing a deep channel in their relationship down which all conflict pours.

Learn How to Stop and Be Stopped

It's worth repeating—"it is your job to stop the process." This is particularly important because a Nice Person is used to hoping that their partner will read their mind. Whether the partner is communicating poorly (threatening, accusing, whining), or whether they are doing a great job of saying their heart's honest truth, there are times when it becomes impossible to listen any more. To pretend to listen, or to wait until we are enraged or devastated, is dishonest and harmful. This is the time to intervene. Some version of the following words should suffice: "I'm sorry, but I can't listen right now. I need some time alone. I need to finish this later."

There is a corollary rule to stopping the process: when one person stops, both stop. A common mistake occurs when the overwhelmed listener asks their partner to stop, only to begin with his or her own issues. The partner is likely to feel misled or manipulated, and the all-important element of trust is undermined.

If you cannot be present with what is being said, it is your job to stop the process

Sanctuary

At this point, both the listener and the talker may need to seek sanctuary. Sanctuary, in this case, is a temporary refuge from further conflict. Couples may need to develop a signal, which may be as simple as saying "sanctuary," that indicates the need to stop and be left alone. The couple must have a prior agreement that when either of them signals "sanctuary" the request must be honored.

This can be incredibly difficult to do. If you are the talker and you have been opening your heart and baring your most intimate feelings, the sudden departure of your listener can feel devastating. You may feel as though you are being abandoned, or that your inner self is so loathsome that your partner could not bear to be with you. Or suppose you have listened quietly and compassionately, and now that it is your turn, you are being cut off. This can feel painfully unfair.

When this happens, it is extremely important to take care of yourself. Take a vigorous walk, meditate, hit a punching bag, curl up with a book, watch some basketball, or wash the dishes. Whatever the activity, it must sufficiently move you away from the passion of the moment so that you can come back to the conflict with a measure of equanimity. You cannot be responsible for your partner's feelings, but you can be responsible for yourself. Now is the time to draw on your resources to comfort yourself. When both partners develop this ability, the relationship is immeasurably stronger.

RULES OF SANCTUARY:
- Don't overuse it
- Make plans to resume the conflict

Beating a Dead Horse . . . Again

Many couples experience the problem of talking an issue into the ground. A conflict may start out well, but by the end there is a sense of being exhausted and having solved nothing. This is often a function of not feeling heard, which may be the result of either or both people not listening well. Good listening is crucial to successful creative conflict.

Another possibility is expecting conflict resolution to involve one person agreeing with the other's point of view. It is not uncommon for a couple to simply have differing opinions that no amount of conflict will resolve. When this happens, it is the couple's job to work out a way to live with their differences and respect one another for being honest.

Creative conflict does not require agreement

Another problem is not realizing when a conflict has been satisfactorily completed. All kinds of interesting feelings get in the way of a couple saying, "Well, I think we've covered most of it. Let's finish this another time." Often, former Nice People can't get over a nagging feeling of wrongness if a conflict is not neatly resolved. The feeling, when traced back, usually has its roots in—"If we disagree, my partner will stop loving me and will probably leave me." Truth is, a good relationship can stand and should be built to incorporate disagreements. In fact, if the major points have been touched on, details can and should be left on the table. If they are important they will stick around and can always be discussed another time. As often as not, they will be forgotten within a week.

Conversely, it is a wonderful feeling to take care of a portion of a conflict and then schedule the rest for later, while the couple is still fresh and feeling good. This is a skillful creative conflict session that will make each partner proud of the other.

Partners Who Won't Dance

Attempting to share honest feelings and thoughts with a person who is not interested in changing will be stultifying at the least, and very likely devastating. At some point a choice has to be made between hiding from the partner (pretending we have not changed), constantly confronting the partner (repeated unproductive conflict), or leaving the partner. Many of us got into relationships with people who wanted us exactly because we were worshipful and always willing to give. Now, we are changing, and our partners may not want to lose the Nice Person that they signed up for.

PASSION AND JOY

Once we get the hang of creative conflict, an amazing thing starts to happen—relationships that were previously unsatisfactory or stale start to get more exciting. In the short term, the relationship gets bouncier, lighter, sexier. Why? Well, for one thing, unspoken issues hang around like an invisible cloud, poisoning the atmosphere. Any sparks we try to strike in the thick air of resentment and suppressed emotion are immediately snuffed out. When the air is clearer, a spark has plenty of oxygen to kindle the fire of romance.

The opening quote of the chapter says, "I vow that I will defend the integrity of my separate being and respect the integrity of your being." This respect is built through creative conflict and it generates a sensuous tension. Not only can the partner be trusted with intimacy, but they are respected as an opposite—a sparring partner, someone whose mettle is worth testing, not only in a conflict but in the bed. It's a clear-sighted kind of passion which allows quick laughter and open enjoyment. Moreover, the couple that has learned how to do creative conflict is an excellent position to communicate freely and with less fear about their sexual needs and preferences.

Pilgrims, Together

Ultimately, creative conflict is not just about solving the budget or toilet seat issues. It is about assisting one another in becoming stronger, happier, and better people. We are all pilgrims on our own journeys. Creative conflict makes it possible to journey together.

With practice, the couple will discover an ascending, mutually reinforcing pattern. When one person opens up a little bit and is able to access a truth—perhaps something they couldn't admit to before—it creates a beautiful, spacious quality. The other partner in turn feels beckoned, perhaps even challenged, to step up, whether it is with a compliment or an acknowledgement or a caress. Now the original partner feels inspired once again. This gentle volleying may take place in a moment or over weeks or months. It may be as subtle as the ability to feel and mirror energy, or as overtly important as the admission of depression or a sexual desire or the discovery of a true calling.

13

Union

O love, open.
Show me my country.
Take me home.

—WENDELL BERRY

Imagine a beautiful romantic relationship, one that is loving and mature. This union doesn't involve princes on white chargers or goddesses removing their veils. In fact, it doesn't involve a state of constant contentment or never-ending eroticism or nonstop glamour. We have romance novels to paint those pictures and even they remind us that tribulations and darkness must be experienced to enjoy the literary ever after.

So let us imagine that it is two Transforming People (or a Transforming Person and a partner who is committed to personal growth), with all their anxiety and defensiveness and past failures, who are in love. Can these two people have an exciting romantic union?

CONTAINERS

Before we explore that question, let's revisit containers. We've talked about a container that allows us to experience our emotions without reflexively acting them out. In a relationship, partners can also build a joint container big enough to hold the relationship. This container does not insulate the couple, but allows them to sample all that the outside world has to bring (money and peaches and children and auto accidents and dogs and vacations in Italy). It also has room for all of the couples' experiences, whether painful (anxiety, sadness, annoyance, ignorance, and bullheadedness) or joyous (the light in their eyes, their laughter, tenderness, admiration, loyalty, patience, eroticism, and spirit). Think of it as a bubble created and maintained by the love and maturity of the couple. Each mindful breath the couple breathes keeps the bubble filled.

So, can we imagine Transforming People having a beautiful romantic union? Yes, very much so. The question is: How do they pull that off?

STATE OF THE UNION

In a Transforming Relationship, both members of the couple are committed to supporting each other's and his or her own transformation. A union is something more than that. In a union, the couple commits to consciously creating an environment in which the relationship can take root and grow. A union acquires a life of its own which, if nurtured properly, can embody a self-sustaining joy and passion.

YOU ARE SO HOT

"Sure, you love him; but are you in love with him?" Most of us have heard phrases like this and we intuitively know what they mean. We can love a person out of years of friendship, respect, gratitude, and loyalty. But do they make our hearts sing? Do we find their collarbone unnervingly sexy? Do they smell delicious? These spontaneous urges are what initially draw us to partners. We call it chemistry and that may, in fact, be exactly what it is. Is there something in their pheromones that particularly lock onto our receptors? Do their emotional rhythms resonate with unconscious echoes of our childhood? How many times have we "fallen" for someone who is incompatible with us or downright unhealthy for us? How many times have we met someone who we knew had all the qualities we had been seeking in a mate, and yet they did not stir our desires?

Union requires the flame of passionate attraction. It's an unpredictable business, however, dealing with fire. The flame may flare and then fizzle—physical attraction fades without corresponding shared beliefs, goals, or commitment. It may be hidden—two old friends may discover passion after many years of platonic relationship. It may be smothered—inflicting and receiving damage or neglect can quickly snuff out attraction.

For the remainder of this chapter, we'll talk about couples who have the flame of attraction and are committed to each other's transformation, and we'll address the question: How do they create a *union*?

TENDING THE GARDEN

Isn't it inevitable that people grow tired of one another? Why do couples get in a rut? Where does the passion go? When people change, won't they necessarily grow apart?

To answer these questions we'll employ that ancient metaphor, the garden. Each partner is a gardener. Their relationship (their attraction and their commitment to one another) is the garden. We know what happens when gardens are neglected; weeds and insects move in, and the flowers and vegetables die. In a season or two the garden is so overrun that the thought of cleaning it up is overwhelming. Sometimes it seems like it would be easier to move to a new plot of land or give up gardening altogether.

What works is persistent and loving tending. Not hyper-vigilance, mind you. A good gardener knows that some weeds and insects are inevitable, and that weather is unpredictable, and that some seeds will take root and some will not. There is an ebb and flow to tending a garden—sometimes it requires hours of work in the hot sun, and sometimes it involves stretching out in a hammock with a cool glass of lemonade and enjoying the view.

What follows are various methods for tending a relationship. Our tool shed is already well stocked with the 7 Practices. What we will show is how loving couples use the practices to create a sustainable and joyous union.

The Couple Embraces Each Other's Needs and Vulnerabilities

Each of us is needy at times; each of us is vulnerable at times; and the condition of anxious attachment amplifies these feelings. It is essential that we have compassion for our neediness without wallowing in it.

Learning to embrace a partner's vulnerabilities is crucial to a union, but the acceptance must start within ourselves. Transforming People often find it much more difficult to embrace their own weaknesses, and will sometimes deflect the acceptance being offered by their beloved. We must learn to accept that we are worthy of our partner's support.

> **We must learn to accept that we are worthy of our partner's support**

When a partner becomes vulnerable or needy (as they inevitably will), it can set off a thousand alarms in the Transforming Person's heart. Through Awareness Practice we can trace the alarms back to our own reactions. Anxiety whispers in our heads, "I hate when he complains about his credit card bill. Why can't he can't take care of himself? I don't want to be responsible for everything!" Awareness Practice says, "I'm picking up on his anxiety about the credit card bill. It makes me anxious and in turn I feel angry at him. But I don't have to take on his nervous energy right now." Watching our own needs and vulnerabilities with compassion allows us to watch our partner's without freaking out.

Sometimes both partners are needy or vulnerable at the same time and have very little reserve to help one another. There are times in a relationship when we must take care of our own needs. Having spent time in the desert we know that we can return as necessary, and that we are ultimately accountable for our own well-being.

As adults, we can heal the anxiety of our childhood by working with a partner to embrace each other's needs and vulnerabilities. Consider what this kind of mutually supportive exchange might look like: When he supports her in her time of need, she grows more certain of herself. This new certainty allows her to see his vulnerability without fear and let him know that she is behind him 100 percent. He allows himself to accept her support without criticizing himself, which strengthens his Warrior Practice. She senses his confidence and feels that for the first time in her life she is in a true partnership. He realizes that, for the first in his life, he is not responsible for both his and his partner's emotional well-being.

There is no end to this upward spiral of mutual support. Embracing both our own and our partner's needs and vulnerabilities is like adding nutrients to the garden soil. Each partner starts growing and the garden begins to bloom.

Recognizing and Embracing Separateness

Here's a typical scenario that contains some clues about the relationship of separateness to passion:

> For some time Lonny and Gabrielle have been getting on each other's nerves. Their rhythm feels off, both in conversation and lovemaking. Lonny is considering breaking up and Gabrielle begs him not to leave.
>
> Over the next few days, Gabrielle comes to terms with the idea of breaking up, locating within herself a place of peace and compassion. She tells Lonny that she is okay with separating.
>
> Now, Lonny is noticing Gabrielle's self-possession. He finds it both comforting and irresistibly sexy. Suddenly, he realizes how deeply he loves Gabrielle and that he can't afford to lose her. Tears flow, truths are told, intimacy flowers, and passion ignites once again.

Gabrielle is not playing hard to get. Though she is feeling grief, her Desert Practice helps her to get more comfortable with her own separateness, and she realizes that she can be okay on her own. Grounded in her separateness, Gabrielle's true character shines. As soon as Lonny gets a look at Gabrielle in this light, he remembers who she is and why he loves her. The fire is rekindled.

A couple may have respect, tenderness, and admiration for one another. They may even have good sexual chemistry. But if one or both of them are Nice People there will also be clinging, ingratiating, neediness, and anxiety, and these qualities throw the proverbial wet blanket on the flame of desire. There is nothing sexier than a partner who is committed to their work, who enjoys their free time, who is unafraid to show their passion for us, who relishes our love. When anxiety is no longer clouding a Transforming Person's heart they not only stop transmitting their fear, but they are free to receive incoming messages as well. Couples in union develop an ease about their relationship that is facilitated by their openness to change.

If a couple is working consciously together on transformation, their ongoing passion grows to the beat of their personal growth. For instance:

> Gary is a Transforming Man. He has always been uncomfortable letting his wife, Jewel, know that he wants to have sex. He's fine if she makes the first move, but he is deeply afraid of the possibility of being rejected and thus has trouble initiating. Jewel wants nothing more than to be carried away by Gary's passion. She has mistaken his reticence for a lack of sexual interest, which makes her feel unattractive and unloved.
>
> As Gary and Jewel begin to work with the 7 Practices, they find that for the first time they are able to discuss these delicate issues. Once they understand each other's fears, the situation no longer seems impossible.
>
> Now they are starting a new pattern: Jewel lets Gary know that she appreciates his advances, the bolder the better. Gary works up his nerve and expresses his sexual interest. Jewel encourages him, and the fire between them builds.

In the example above, Jewel and Gary have created a mutual support situation in which the tending of their relationship affects their personal growth and vice versa. As Jewel compliments Gary's advances, he becomes more self-assured. Jewel finds Gary's confidence to be sexy and his attention makes her feel attractive and loved. Jewel and Gary are helping each other become less anxious and more secure.

A question that we asked above is whether it is inevitable that people grow tired of one another. One of the secrets of ongoing desire is found in the word "transforming." Transforming People are constantly changing; generating self-love, new insights, personal excitement, and productivity separately from their partner. This allows them to bring a constantly renewed sense of enthusiasm and interest to a relationship. The process of discovery is, in good part, what generates the initial heat of falling in love. When both partners are changing, there is always something new to be discovered.

Separateness must go hand-in-hand with merger. Most Nice People long for merger, but find separateness painful. In union, we want to flow from separateness to merger and back, without feeling anxious. In garden terms, we are honoring each season as it arrives, and this mindful tending results in rare flowers of passion at unexpected times.

The ability to flow from separateness to merger and back generates ongoing passion

The Couple Practices a Conscious Commitment to Honesty and Trust

Honesty and trust are the paramount qualities for tending a union. A romantic relationship can withstand insensitivity, failure, meanness, niceness, etc., but dishonesty and distrust are killers. Neither honesty nor trust is fast-growing—each requires time and care.

Honesty in this context means much more than simply "not lying." It is the capacity to face difficult truths and the strength to act with integrity even when it involves pain or fear. Trust requires two partners who are each tending to their own honesty, as well as examining their own sources of distrust. Trust follows honesty the way one season follows the next.

Our seminal experiences of honesty and trust come from our family. The more thoroughly we understand our family history, the more clearly we will be able to see our patterns of dishonesty and distrust. This can be as overt as "my father cheated on my mother and now I'm cheating on my wife." It can also be intricate and subtle. "My mother was terrified of me being hurt or going through loss and so she tried to fix everything for me. And if she couldn't fix it, she minimized it. Now I have trouble admitting when something is wrong. I pretend everything's okay so I won't cause problems for anyone else."

As adults, the Goddess/Prince Construct is the most powerful instigator of dishonesty. To please (or keep) the Goddess/Prince, Nice People will exaggerate, obfuscate, hide, stonewall, prevaricate, dodge, deflect, and deny, not to mention lie and cheat. Family and Disillusionment Practices are keys to developing honesty and trust in a union.

When we start trusting ourselves, it becomes possible to start trusting our partner

Years of repeating the same thought processes, of harboring the same secret fears, of constructing illusions, can make them part of the fabric of our consciousness. It is hard to know sometimes when we are not being honest with ourselves. It is hard to know, after years of distrusting everyone, or trusting the wrong people, when we have met someone who deserves our trust. The Brotherhood and Sisterhood are there to hold up the mirror that reaffirms our honesty and calls out our dishonesty. They are the indispensable second and third opinion on whether our trust is warranted or unwarranted, miserly or overly generous.

Nonjudgmental awareness is a form of honesty. Watching our bodies, feelings, thoughts, and actions allows us to understand why we do what we do and how it affects our relationship.

"Yesterday when we were talking, you interrupted me, but I did my Nice Girl thing and didn't mention it; and then I was mad at you the rest of the afternoon. Anyway, that's why things were tense. I should have spoken up right away."

"I was wondering what was going on. I'm sorry for interrupting you. And thanks for figuring that out. You're pretty amazing."

While this bit of honesty may seem a slight thing, when it is compounded with a thousand more moments of honesty it creates a solid wall of trust that surrounds and protects the union. It is as if, even amid the rush of daily life, the union is tucked away in a safe haven of moss-covered stones and sweet running water.

All Relationships End

A relationship may end in a parting of ways, in a divorce, or in the death of one of the partners, but end it will. This is upsetting to Nice People who are terrified of experiencing the emotions associated with breaking up and being alone. There can also be an element of humiliation in ending a relationship because much of our society esteems only life-long marriage, and brands anything else a failure. Nice People often swear unconditional love (or at least yearn for it) in an attempt to ease these anxieties and manufacture the security they did not receive in childhood.

But relationships *are* conditional. They are conditioned upon certain standards of behavior and continuing shared goals and values. Violence, abuse, infidelity, divergent ethics, mental and/or emotional instability, addiction—all of these and more may be conditions for ending a relationship. So too may the glacial divides of boredom and alienation. Furthermore, life-long marriage as the sole acceptable model for a successful relationship is out of step with the way most people live today. Statistically, serial monogamy is the norm in our society, and the length of a relationship is no measure of its quality.

There is an enormous paradox hidden here. Nice People suppress their urge to change or help their partner change because they are afraid that change will lead to losing their partner. But this very inactivity causes the death of the relationship.

When a couple is grounded in the awareness that their relationship will end, it becomes possible to commit fully to the relationship, not out of fear of separation, but out of the genuine desire to be with the other person. Admitting this hard reality allows the couple to be truthful with one another. In this environment of open transformation the couple is not only more likely to stay together until "death do us part," but more likely to be excited and passionate the entire way. And should they part ways sooner, they have a good chance to do so with dignity and grace.

Contemplating the end of the relationship allows for:
1. Honesty without the paralyzing fear of losing the relationship
2. Choosing the relationship, not submitting to it

As a Transforming Person's anxiety begins to subside, the possibility of ending a union becomes less terrifying. Certainly, there will be pain and grief. There may be anger. But there is no longer the Nice Person's terror of experiencing those emotions. Furthermore, the Transforming Person has already come to terms with the fear of being alone. This allows the couple to engage in creative conflict, and the result is a healthy growing union.

Contemplating the end of a relationship provides a litmus test for the worth and quality of the relationship

Now the couple can bring up topics, whether large or small, that may rock the boat of the relationship. This is a job for two warriors who not only exhibit courage but also invite the courage of their lover. Truth leads to growth, and, as we have already seen, growth fosters ongoing passion. Transforming People, then, must learn to do a kind of high-wire act in which they sponsor their partner's change while letting go of the fear that their partner will leave.

The good news is that this high-wire act, along with sometimes being scary, is thrilling and beautiful and satisfying. Instead of hiding what is sensitive in a relationship because we are afraid of angering the Goddess/Prince, we take the risk of bringing it out into the light. "I want more excitement in our lives, but you don't seem to have the same ambition." "Sometimes I wish you could be more feminine." "I don't like being a parent." "I'm thinking about changing professions." Any one of these statements could lead to the end of a relationship, but if they are *not* spoken the relationship will surely end, though more slowly and painfully. And yet, once the words are spoken and the risk is taken, there is an enormous opportunity for the couple to support one another, and facilitate incredible growth.

Restraint must also play an important role in a successful union. **When we talk about the courage to be honest, we are not suggesting that every desire or concern a person has must be examined and pursued.** For instance, the statement, "I don't like being a parent," is frightening and should not be spoken lightly. Usually, such a statement means that a partner is at the end of his or her rope and is asking for help. They know that they have a duty to be a good parent. They know that if they suffer in silence, things will get worse. So they risk frightening their partner in the hopes of finding a way to work on the problem.

Landscaping and mulching are the gardener skills at work in this section. Without the clinging fear of losing our loved one, we are free to experiment. We can clear the dense undergrowth to allow sunlight in, opening up space for the union to flourish. We enrich our passion with truth, courage, and respect for our partner, and wait to see what new kind of relationship will result.

The Interplay of the Masculine and the Feminine

We have talked about femininity and masculinity as the personal experience of one's own gender. Shedding our niceness, we find ourselves wearing a new skin. It is tougher than the last one, yet more flexible and sensitive. We are able to experience a wider range of emotions, physical sensations, and thoughts. When it comes to gender, the anxious-to-please world of the Nice Person tends toward either neutrality or an exaggerated and often uncomfortable role-playing. The open, strong world of the Transforming Person allows us to embrace masculinity and/or femininity more naturally and fully.

In the safe container of a union, the couple is able to enthusiastically inhabit maleness and femaleness. The interplay and tension between the two is delicious and makes us feel alive. This is about flirting and sex, and it's about everyday life, too. It doesn't matter who is masculine or who is feminine or how much or when. The only guidelines are as follows:

- Act from a genuine place inside yourself
- Communicate with your partner
- Encourage your partner's exploration
- Be willing to tell your partner when their way of acting feminine or masculine feels uncomfortable or inappropriate to you

Here are some examples of masculine and feminine interplay:

- "I love taking over in bed and running the show. But sometimes, I wish you would run the show, and I could be taken."
- "I like when you bring me a cup of coffee when I'm working."
- "Thank you for stepping in and defending me back there. It makes me feel very safe when you do that."
- "You're running a fever. Get in bed. I'll take care of everything."
- "Hold me here, like this. And firm; don't worry, you won't hurt me. That's right"
- "Baby, I got the job! I'm so excited for our future!"
- "Mmm, I like when you look at me that way."

These exchanges are each particular to an individual, and in some instances it is impossible to tell whether the speaker's experience is masculine or feminine. Each of us has a blend of femininity and masculinity that is unique to us. In a union, we get to discover our own blend in counterpoint to our partner's blend. If the environment is safe, and if each partner encourages the other, the union becomes a delightful playground. This is the summer part of the garden—strawberries ripe to bursting and full of sunshine, fresh corn and beans and tomatoes—the harvest and even the feast after the harvest.

HUMOR, GRACE, AND PATIENCE REDUX

The satisfaction of laughing together, the tolerance and forgiveness that exemplify grace, and the gift of patience—all are crucial in a romantic union. There is a beautiful irony that these qualities, which were once employed in the service of our compulsive niceness, now serve as essential nutrients for a union. When humor, grace, and patience flow through a relationship, the union is infused with depth and sweetness.

ENERGETICS

As we practice awareness of ourselves, so can we practice awareness of our relationships. This awareness is not primarily the product of the logical brain. "Ah, by my lover's reaction, I deduce that I have communicated my displeasure in an underhanded manner and thus have engendered her own ire." No, mostly we *feel* in a relationship. Something feels on or it feels off. One moment we're rowing smoothly and in unison, pleased with each other and the world, and the next we're paddling in opposite directions, growing annoyed and getting nowhere. We're feeling the energetics of the relationship.

This is known as limbic resonance, the emotional communication system that we share with all mammals. Our first connections with our mother, before our brains could formulate thought, are limbic resonance. As we stared into her face, we received and gave back thousands of limbic messages that aided us in our learning and growth. As adults, we are still communicating with our partners via the same system. Energy flows from our lovers to us and back again, and as it does it has a profound effect on our personal energy.

Everything we have written about in this book can be viewed as energetics. The 7 Practices are methods for gauging and adjusting our energy. Anxious attachment is like having a faulty energetic connection somewhere in our being. Unfortunately, we can't just replace the whole psyche, so we keep tinkering and tuning. In the last three chapters, we have been working with methods for adjusting the energetics of a relationship.

In many romantic relationships, the participants don't even know that there *is* energy because they are not attuned to it. When they do notice that something is wrong, it is often after damage is done, and even *then* they don't have the tools to do anything about it.

In a union, we start to get good at recognizing energetics. Our diagnostic equipment becomes very sensitive—sometimes we can even feel the shift in the energy as it happens. We have a pretty good idea of what is gumming up the works and we've got some great tools for getting everything back to running smoothly. When we "tend the garden," we are tuning the limbic resonance in the union. Thomas Lewis says: ". . . love alters the structure of our brains." He does not only mean this poetically or metaphorically, he means that love changes the physical structure of the brain. In other words, through the loving intimacy of a union we can repair the damage done by anxious attachment and move towards wholeness.

14

Stand by Your Transforming Man or Woman

Love does not consist in gazing at each other, but in looking together in the same direction.

—ANTOINE DE SAINT-EXUPERY

Despite the familiar tales of instantaneous change involving genies, sorcerers, and fairy godmothers, the process of genuine transformation takes time to unfold. Those who are working to heal from chronic anxiety are no exception. Their journey is difficult, and their rewards are vast.

If your partner is such a person, you have your own set of challenges to navigate. You also stand to benefit greatly from the ways in which your partner is becoming more calm, more open, and more loving. This chapter has been written specifically for you, offering direction and insight that is designed to assist you through this process. This will not only help you survive, but will show how you can foster healing and growth in your partner, your relationship, and yourself. We encourage you to adopt only what makes sense to you at this time, keeping in mind that an idea that doesn't apply now may be quite useful at a later date.

YOUR MINDSET MATTERS

When working on relationship issues, your own state of mind can be either an asset or a liability. We are complex creatures, capable of feeling many different emotions and holding many different attitudes at once. It is important to be conscious and intentional about your mindset.

Mindset #1: Be Cool

Your partner's process of change can be a virtual roller coaster of fears, hopes, struggles, and breakthroughs. It can be very uncomfortable to be pulled along on that wild ride, even more so if you grew up in a family that was chaotic or anxious. There is often a temptation during tempestuous times to try to enforce some kind of peace, pushing your partner to feel differently than they do. As you may already have discovered, that doesn't work so well. If your partner is in the early part of their work, they may react with familiar Nice Person behavior—appeasing, apologizing, and acquiescing, followed (perhaps) by passive-aggressive behavior. If your partner is further along in the process, he or she may be able to talk with you about how it feels when you push, or ask you to speak your mind about what is making you uncomfortable.

Mindset #2: Be Clear

Another dynamic is the pull to be the "Rock" or the "Saint"—that person who is tirelessly patient and understanding, seeming to have no needs of their own—an amalgam of Albert Schweitzer, Florence Nightingale, and Mr. Rogers.

As heroic as that may sound, you and your partner may both be more hamstrung than helped by your determination to be incredible. Efforts to overfunction for a recovering Nice Person can lead them to (a) compete with you for the role of "hero," and/or (b) let go of responsibility and just let you take care of everything. Neither of these are good outcomes.

The alternative is to be clear with yourself and your partner. Your primary responsibility is your own life, and it is up to you to decide how to manage that life. This includes developing an ongoing awareness of what you need, what you need to be doing, and what you have to offer at any given time.

Imagine, for example, that you're feeling depleted from working long hours on your job and fighting off the flu. You need to be getting extra sleep and having more quiet time to yourself. You're about to head off to bed when your partner comes to you and says that she or he is feeling really insecure and wants to talk. You know that talks like this can be exhausting, and immediately you feel torn between your desire to be supportive and your need for rest. It will be much better for both of you if you can tell your partner what you need and what you have to offer—and then stick to your guns! You might say, "I would love to listen to you right now, but I'm worn out and don't have a lot to give. Would it help for me to hold you for a few minutes and then we can talk first thing in the morning?"

This setting of boundaries and limits is not only good for you, it's good for your partner as well. They need to be able to feel where the edges are, to know that you won't give too much and then resent them later for it. They need to know that you will trust them to manage their own life. If you rescue your partner, you undermine their confidence by communicating that they can't handle it and need you to bail them out. By being clear about your own limits you are sending an important message to your partner: "I believe you can do this yourself."

Mindset #3: Be Kind

Kindness in words creates confidence
Kindness in thinking creates profoundness
Kindness in giving creates love.

—LAO TZU

Just about everything in life is made better with kindness. Kindness gives meaning to a phrase or gesture, elevates conversation, softens a disappointment, and sweetens a celebration. In an intimate relationship, these effects are amplified with the daily practice of kindness toward your partner as well as yourself.

To explain what we mean by "kindness," it helps to explain what it *isn't*. Being kind is not the same as being "nice." Niceness is about trying to make things go smoothly, trying to "grease the skids." Niceness usually involves being polite, making sure you're not ruffling any feathers or disturbing the peace. The purpose of kindness isn't to make things go smoother—it's to make things better. An act of kindness might very well ruffle feathers or disturb the peace, but it will come from a loving intent.

The kindness that may have the most impact in your relationship is the practice of grace. To practice grace means to make room for a person, for who they really are and what they feel. This doesn't mean that you approve of everything they do—grace is not a license to act badly. Grace is the act of receiving someone in whatever condition you find them.

It is important to practice grace toward yourself as much as with your partner. You may find that you wish you didn't feel a certain way, didn't have particular habits, could be more patient, or had a better comprehension of what your partner was thinking. Recognizing a desire for change is great, but the process of change needs to start with kindness toward yourself. When you are at war with your own thoughts and feelings, it's hard to be able to study them or express them clearly. When you begin with grace, it is much easier to notice what's going on inside of you and to do something about it.

SUPPORTING YOUR PARTNER'S TRANSFORMATION

It is a wonderful thing to be committed to helping your partner through whatever difficulty they are facing; indeed, one of the features of a Transforming Relationship is that the partners support each other's growth process. The tricky matter, of course, is figuring out how to do that. Efforts to help don't always make things better, and sometimes the right thing to do isn't what you would expect. Here are a few things you can do to support your partner.

Learn about Anxious Attachment and the Process of Transformation

If you can understand what your partner is wrestling with, where it comes from, and what heals it, you will have already done a tremendously loving thing. Your partner has to do the work and you can't rescue them from that. But by getting a feel for what they're dealing with and what they're heading for, you are letting them know that they're not in this alone.

There are many sources for learning about this, and two of them are readily available: your partner and this book. Your partner can tell you their personal experience about how things work for him or her, while *Anxious to Please* gives you both an overview and helpful tips. Three topics are particularly important for you to learn about:

- Your partner's chronic anxiety—where it comes from, what it feels like
- Your partner's chronic niceness—what they do and why
- Your partner's path of transformation—what they're trying to do differently and why

Be in Touch with Your Partner's Process

Your partner is engaged in a major renovation, a project similar to getting a graduate degree or training for the Olympics. It is a big part of their life and their future, and it's important for you to know what they are working on for several reasons:

- **It communicates caring.** Your interest in your partner's process shows that you care about their growth and happiness and that you want to walk through this with them.
- **It helps you to know what to expect.** Your partner will be making changes to the ways that they think and act, including the ways that they act in their relationship with you. This is likely to be clumsy at times, but understanding their intentions will help make sense of their actions.
- **It enhances your own growth.** The various concepts, techniques, and strategies that your partner is working with may be tailored for them,

but many of these resources will be of great use to anyone. The more you learn about your partner's process, the more you'll learn about yourself and your own path of development.

- **It's an investment in your future together.** The process of transformation doesn't ever end, but it usually has an arc. After a period of intense growth and change, there is often a tapering. The new life becomes more normal, and there is a settling in. By being intimately involved with your partner's process, you are traveling along the road with them, strengthening your relationship every step of the way.

Notice, Encourage, and Compliment Progress

Professional athletes appreciate the "intelligent fan"—the person who understands the subtleties of the game enough to know when to cheer and when not to. Musicians and stage actors say the same thing about insightful audiences who understand when to be silent and when to applaud.

Anytime we are going through something difficult, it can be a drink of cool water to be reminded that someone who loves us is rooting us on. Your partner is working through something that will feel painful, discouraging, and confusing. You may wish at times that you could run this marathon for them or rescue them from it, but of course you cannot. What you can do is witness them, understand what they're going through, and celebrate their accomplishments with them.

Expect Your Partner to Be Setting Boundaries

People who are chronically nice have a tough time with boundaries. They are afraid that they will mess up important relationships if they say "No" or "I'd like to do such-and-such" or "I feel differently about it than you." Setting boundaries, then, is a crucial skill for them to learn, and the place they are most likely to practice it is (you guessed it) with you.

Unfortunately, people who are learning to set boundaries are usually pretty awkward at first. One time they will be too meek about it and will be discouraged that you didn't get their signal; on another try, they will do it too emphatically, and it may be difficult for you to respond without being defensive. In some relationships *both* people are learning to set boundaries and can really struggle for a while until they begin to get good at it.

You can expect your partner's emotions (particularly insecurity) to be running high when they are practicing setting boundaries. It may not make a lot of sense on the surface—after all, you might reason, they have no cause to be upset or worried—but try to remember that they have been afraid of rejection and abandonment since they were little. The "simple" act of disagreeing with you probably feels utterly hazardous to them, even if consciously they know that it's not. Their greatest reassurance comes as they discover that it is, in fact, safe to disagree, ask for what they want, express their disappointment, or just say no.

Support Your Partner's Healthy Same-Gender Friendships

Men and women alike need good friendships with people of the same gender (we refer to these friendships as the Brotherhood and Sisterhood—see Chapter Seven). These relationships provide a unique kind of sustenance that is particularly needed by Nice People.

People who are healing from anxious attachment may have a pattern of trying to get all of their needs met from their partner—one-stop shopping—and will let go of important friendships once they are in a long-term relationship. Many Nice People are afraid that their partner won't like it if they develop their own Sisterhood or Brotherhood.

Your partner needs to feel your support for their healthy same-gender friendships. It is up to them to develop these relationships, but you can help by encouraging them and by being understanding about the time it takes to get together with these people. Keep in mind that men and women often go about these friendships in different ways, and that your partner may not pursue them in the same way you would.

It is important to note that we are emphasizing *healthy* same-gender friendships. It isn't useful (or honest) to pretend to support friendships that you don't think are good for your partner. People need friends who are sufficiently mature and capable of compassion and good judgment.

TAKE CARE OF YOURSELF TOO

There are *two* people in your relationship, and both of you are of equal importance. It is terrific that you want to support your partner through this time, but it is just as essential that you take good care of yourself. What's good for the goose is good for the gander, as they say, and the best plan is for both of you to get what you need. Here are a few ideas for your own self-care:

- **Take care of yourself physically.** Everything—your mind, emotions, intuition, etc.—everything works better when your body is healthy. Pay attention to exercise, diet, and sleep.
- **Develop your own healthy same-gender friendships.** For all of the reasons mentioned earlier. When you're supporting someone else, you need support too.
- **Join a support group.** You may not think you're a "support-group-kind-of-person," but there are lots of variations to check out.
- **Do a course of psychotherapy.** Get a private and safe environment to talk with someone who is well-trained, experienced, and is there for just one reason—you.

A WORD OF ENCOURAGEMENT

Relationships are wonderful, and they're also messy and complicated—all the more so when your partner is going through a major change. It isn't possible to do it perfectly, and you'll make yourself nutty if you try.

You are going to experience frustration, disappointment, and confusion to go along with the excitement, contentment, and clarity. Do your best to enjoy the ride and see the humor in it. There's no better way to support your partner, deepen your relationship, and improve your life.

Epilogue

Fall down seven times, get up eight.

—DARUMA DAISHI

Transformation generates its own momentum. Patterns of self-care that used to seem as uncomfortable as a scratchy wool sweater are starting to feel more like your favorite flannel shirt. Confrontations that once tied your innards in knots now only stir a few butterflies. Friendships are deeper and more satisfying, and things might even be looking better in the romance department. Areas of life that felt barren and disjointed are beginning to thrive and coalesce. Every dimension of life is fostering growth from every other dimension.

People who have undergone life-changing transformations all have one thing in common: they didn't quit. When you feel discouraged, overwhelmed, fatigued, or even desperate, your main job is to persist. Everything else follows. As Winston Churchill once said, "If you are going through hell, keep going."

Every person that embarks on a path of transformation forges a new trail. We can be supported, guided, and inspired by those who have gone before us, but we must each find our own way.

Therein lies a mystery about our lifelong attachment wound. The real rupture is the one that keeps us from ourselves. There never was anyone else to please. The love we sought was here all the time, waiting for us to come home.

Index

A

yes yes

About the Authors

© Jerry Davis

James Rapson, M.S., LMFT, is a clinical member of the American Association of Marriage and Family Therapists, the U.S. Association of Body Psychotherapists, and the Center for Object Relations in Seattle. Mr. Rapson is a veteran therapist who combines hard-won personal insight with clinical experience and scholarship. The journey of healing and growth in his own life has been greatly amplified by the courageous men and women with whom he has the privilege to work. Mr. Rapson's focus on human connection, coupled with his penchant for innovation, has led him to develop programs such as Group of Dads, Couples in Motion, and The Shared Vision Project. James' collaboration with Craig has led to the development of numerous seminars, workshops, and classes.

An avid learner, James draws from a diverse background that includes early career forays in the worlds of music, software engineering, theater, and religion, as well as even earlier exploits on the football field and wrestling mat. These days his wrestling is mostly limited to matters of the mind and heart, though he continues to play piano, write poetry, and take the occasional raft trip down a northwest river. He has a private practice in Bellevue, Washington.

© Jerry Davis

Craig English, M.F.A., is an award-winning writer with extensive experience in both nonfiction and fiction. He is the founder of the much-published "Commoners" writing group in Seattle, Washington. A dynamic lecturer, teacher, and workshop leader, he draws from the wisdom traditions of both East and West to deliver a message that is warm, tough, funny, and poignant.

Mr. English performed as a professional actor for twenty-five years, with numerous credits on stage, television, and radio. He has cofounded such diverse projects as a groundbreaking Montessori middle school and a highly-regarded Shakespearean theater company. Among his interests, Craig counts hiking, kayaking, skiing, drinking tea, cooking, reading, and laughing.

Craig and James first met in 1965 on a grade school playground in Santa Barbara, California, and discovered that they shared a similar offbeat sense of humor. They have marked the stages of life together with comic books and ping-pong marathons, dreams of kissing the perfect girl and becoming rock stars, college hijinks and geographical relocations, through buying homes, raising children, and earning some gray hairs along the way. They are, forty years later, still best friends.